# I Just Want to

# Be Alone

a collection of humorous essays by

Some Super Cool Lady Writers

@throat_punch Books


Copyright 2014 by @throat_punch Books


All rights reserved.

# TABLE OF CONTENTS

# INTRODUCTION

Like most women, I have fantasies. Mine don't involve half naked men and red rooms of pain, though. My fantasies are usually centered around an empty house, a good book, and a hot cup of tea.

A few years ago I made some huge strides towards achieving my fantasy. I managed to get both of my kids into school with the hope that I'd have several hours of uninterrupted alone time to read books and drink tea.

Except I forgot about the one thing that could ruin my plans.

I forgot about the Hubs. I can't send him to school with the kids and he works from home, so there is no escaping him.

I love my husband, but ...

Here are just a few things that I'm not crazy about:

His snoring. It's like sleeping next to a locomotive.

He eats with his mouth open. This doesn't happen all the time, just predominantly in the winter months, when he's suffering from the dreaded "Man Cold" and becomes a mouth breather.

When he licks his lips after every meal. I've been told this is a compliment to my culinary skills, but I'm not buying it. Nothing ruins *my* appetite more than listening to him suck his teeth and smack his lips.

The scratching. Always with the scratching. If it isn't his balls, then it's his butt.

His habit of sniffing the piles of laundry next to the bed to determine the cleanliness of his clothes.

I Just Want to Be Alone

And my favorite: the dry hump in front of the dishwasher. In the immortal words of Amy Flory, "The day my husband doesn't dry hump me from behind while I'm loading the dishwasher is the day that I know it's over."

Ain't that the truth?

     –   Jen of People I Want to Punch in the Throat

# MAYBE PAULA ABDUL WAS RIGHT
## By Nicole Leigh Shaw
### *Ninja Mom Blog*

**Tim:** I'm eagle-eye, daddy! Tell me what you need. I'll find it.
**Kid:** Where's the long thing mommy uses for dusting? The one that's a stick that gets bigger.
**Tim:** (looking in the closet) I don't see it.

It was a typical weekday night in suburbia during which my husband Tim and I were watching a crime show. *Criminal Minds*, I think, but it may have been a *Law and Order* episode or *American Idol*, something that has the potential to cause nightmares. What we didn't actually like, we liked to make fun of, and so we passed the hour armchair quarterbacking fictional crimes. "Oh, like there's that much blood from a severed finger." A certain level of believability is required in a show where a man is carrying around a bag of eyeballs.

We had a lot to poke fun at. There was the terribly written show itself; no fewer than three airings of a commercial featuring a punch line with God's oopsie, man nipples; and a weatherman who teased us with a snowy forecast.

As conversation does when bombarded with bad TV and worse weather, our chat turned south, not to sex organs, but to Florida.

**Me:** I prefer gulf shrimp.
**Tim:** They're tasty. Hey! That's another good reason to move to Florida.
**Me:** So they should drum up residents by pitching "The shrimp are tasty?"
**Tim:** And the grapefruit.
**Me:** The what?
**Tim:** Florida grapefruit.
**Me:** Shrimp and grapefruit?
**Tim:** You like grapefruit.
**Me:** I don't like grapefruit. You lost me at grapefruit.

## I Just Want to Be Alone

The obvious follow-up to shrimp and grapefruit was my recalling that a friend had righteously blasted attachment parent and former child star/current sitcom star Mayim Bialik.

**Me:** Remember that show *Blossom*?
**Tim:** No.
**Me:** —
**Tim:** —
**Me:** Okay.

And so it goes. When you share living space and DNA-hybrids with each other, you need to cover a lot of territory in terms of talk. Non sequitur conversations, quips, and comments that flow out-of-sync with time, are the norm when you've been married for a while. "Would you like milk in your coffee?" turns suddenly to "What's the deal with your mom's mole?" But spouses who've shared a life for any significant length of time can still keep up with the chatter. It's a good metaphor for marriage, generally. One day it's "Do you like this china pattern?" The next day it's "How much money did you say was in the bank account? Only that much? Well, it's not because I bought all those ShamWows. Those are going to pay for themselves!" If you can't keep up with the changing conversation, you're screwed.

It also goes that you're not always going to be on the same page, or even in the same book. My husband and I aren't helped by the fact that we are nearly total opposites. From politics to whether tuna melts are delicious (they are!), we share little more than being human and a tendency to laugh at the same time.

I've been married to my husband for twelve years. Even back when this *Blossom* chat happened and we only had a decade of marriage behind us, I understood that the mark of successful marital dialogue is knowing when a failure to communicate is a sign that the conversation is over—not the marriage. It sounds logical enough, not letting a moment where you don't understand each other signal that it's time to hire a divorce attorney, but I hardly think most about-to-be-weds are logical. I certainly hoped, if not expected, that my groom would be overwhelmed, permanently, by his love and devotion to me. As such, he'd want to know my every thought and see the world from my point-of-view.

I gave up being entirely understood sometime between "I do" and "It's a girl." In fact, I can remember the last time I really cared about my husband seeing things my way.

**Me:** I want you to cut the baby's cord.
**Tim:** Why?
**Me:** Why not?
**Tim:** Because it just seems gross and I can imagine it feels kinda yucky. Like cutting through a wet rubber hose.
**Me:** But you're not doing anything! Nothing to get this baby out! You can at least cut the cord!
**Tim:** I'm pretty sure that's what we pay the doctor for.

At the time I was emotionally compromised, as very pregnant women are, and tired of doing all the heavy lifting and body fluid secreting. I wanted him to do at least one undesirable thing related to birthing a baby. It only seemed fair, if strange and vindictive. Then she was born, our first baby, and I just didn't care anymore because life had happened in every sense of the phrase.

And there we were. Married and dealing with it. We no longer had a marriage outline, the one we'd created when there was only future in front of us and not much actual living behind us. It was a newlyweds' outline: kids, nice-but-modest home, a dog, no shoes in the house, and we'll always kiss goodbye when we leave each other. I guess the outline got lost, or burned, or recycled, or I used the back of it to make a grocery list. The two of us have been relying on instinct, trust, coffee, and Dr. Phil episodes for at least eight years now.

We don't always kiss when we leave each other. Actually, we rarely do. He doesn't bring me flowers, but I don't need them. He does bring me the pound of butter I ask him to pick up, and I do need that. The rest of the time we spend trying to make each other's lives easier, even if that sometimes means getting the hellout of the way. I guess I just don't need Prince Charming anymore. I don't need a spouse who's my everything. I need one who's my most things.

> **Me:** I want you to do the research on football-related head in juries and brain damage and stuff.
> **Tim:** And I'd do that because I love brains?
> **Me:** No, because I researched it and I worry about Roo playing football but I want you to check it out and I want your opinion because I don't want to be a nut about it.
> **Tim:** On a scale of one to ten, how worried are you about this?
> **Me:** I don't want him to play football.
> **Him:** We'll say that's a ten. So, I'll check it all out, but even if I do and I think it's okay and you don't, then he won't play. That's it. You're not going to spend your life dreading every Saturday because he might scramble his brains.

This reasonable, caring soul is the same man who DOESN'T KNOW WHO BLOSSOM IS and never leaves me the Kohl's card when he travels. He doesn't always wrap my gifts, a pet peeve of mine that will someday cause me to commit a felony. I'm leaning toward arson. He is the same guy who avoided, not only cutting the umbilical cord for each of our four children, but also ninety percent of their diaper changes. He hasn't finished painting our mudroom. He doesn't know what I bought his family for Christmas. He went gluten-free two days before wheat's favorite holiday: Thanksgiving. He leaves his socks in the living room. He listens only part of the time when I tell him which kid needs to be where and when. He doesn't know the correct words to most nursery rhymes. He passes gas on the stairs when I'm walking up behind him, on purpose and with great joy. He thinks his Franken-feet are so lovely he could be a foot model. (He is wrong.)

The fact is that sometimes I don't understand him at all; I'm sure the feeling is mutual.

But often enough we do manage agreement, sympathetic acknowledgment, and shared understanding. That's all I need: enough.

Some people describe opposite personalities as being like oil and water. I prefer to think of us as oil and vinegar. You need to whisk us violently together, but we are fabulous over leafy greens.

And, should I still need proof that this man understands me, knows me, and loves me, I have a hand-scrawled note left on the kitchen table a few years ago:

*Nik, I love you! I think you're awesome! –T*

**"It ain't fiction, just a natural fact. We come together 'cause opposites attract."**
**–Paula Abdul**


*NICOLE LEIGH SHAW writes professionally, and with pizazz, for Nick-Mom.com, Mamalode.com, InThePowderRoom.com, Moms.FortWayne.com, and anywhere else that pays in cash.com. She's been featured on Huff-Post Parents and HuffPost Comedy, as well as her mom's fridge. When not writing, you'll find her standing in the kitchen, wondering, "Why did I come into this room?" Once upon a time she was a mostly serious news journalist, an accidental magazine columnist, and a mediocre editor. Now she funnels an enthusiasm for meeting minimum requirements into her blog NinjaMomBlog.com, and finding pairs of socks for her kids that kind of match. With four kids under age ten (two are twins), she can say with confidence that she's finally gotten the hang of this birth control thing: Facebook. Because one cannot procreate and update statuses at the same time.*

# Life With the Thin Guy
## By Kim Forde
### *The Fordeville Diaries*

I'm married to one of those men that women hate. Not because of any personality flaw or anything serious. But because he is that guy: *The effortlessly thin man.*

Yeah, him. We all know someone just like him.

He's the one who eats whatever the hell he wants. The one who does not exercise.

The one who never gains a pound. The one with no appreciation whatsoever of his over-performing metabolism and blue ribbon DNA.

It's a real problem for me. Well, it was – until recently.

With his blessing, I can tell you that my 5'10" husband has consistently weighed between one hundred fifty one and one hundred fifty eight pounds since he was twenty years old. When I say that he was always able to eat *anything*\* and do *zero* exercise without suffering any consequences, I'm honestly not exaggerating. So if you're looking for a place to direct any food/diet-related rage, I have your man right here.

I, on the other hand, have worked very hard for every pound I've ever lost and also seem to possess the unique genetic ability to gain weight merely by visualizing junk food while driving, sleeping, or even running on the treadmill. I have my weaknesses but, on the whole, I eat a balanced and healthy diet. I try to work out a few times a week. Just to avoid gaining weight. Losing any is a bonus. Or a fluke. Or a stomach virus.

So, you'll forgive me if I feel a little giddy about my husband's recent dose of metabolic justice.

------------

*\*To be clear: Yeah, he eats a lot but, I mean, not in a gluttonous way. Not like the guys on the competitive hot dog eating circuit. They're disgusting – he's just lean.*

I should point out that he has not fattened up. He looks great to me. But, at his recent physical, he was surprised to learn he had put on about ten pounds, not long after he had noticed his pants were feeling a little snug. And he was pissed. I want to offer him my empathy, because I know how annoying and disheartening it is to feel that waistband start to threaten your optimal levels of circulation. But I can't. I'm too busy thanking the forces of nature for finally giving him a constitution like most of us mere mortals.

Welcome to the dark side, my friend, where the majority of us have lived for decades. Never mind that you've escaped a designated seat at our table through your mid-forties. We're happy to have you. I'd offer you a muffin, but I exceeded my daily points allowance at about 10:43 this morning. How about six almonds and a black coffee instead?

I know, I know – I should be a more supportive spouse. So I did a few things to demonstrate that, ultimately, I'm in his corner.

First, I totally waited until he left the room to raise my fist in the air in a gesture of joy and victory. I don't *think* my maniacal laugh could be heard outside of my own head, but I can't be 100 percent sure.

Second, and more productively, I put together a short list of things he may want to change if he's looking to drop those ten pounds. Because, let's be honest: It's way more fun to watch someone else go down this road and benefit from a lifetime of knowledge I've begrudgingly accumulated on this topic.

And so I presented him with my suggestions. He has to ditch the following habits, effective rightfuckingnow:

1. Adding any of these items to the family's grocery list: Ring Dings, coffee cake, Entenmann's donuts or the perennial favorite: "Just get us more snack food." In fact, as much as I appreciate any of his offers to do the grocery shopping, I think it may have to stop. It's not fair to the staff of the bakery section to have no warning of his shock-and-awe approach.
2. Calling my entire dinner the size of an appetizer and then

mumbling about how I must be starving.

3. Snorting in disgust at the widely accepted idea of substituting beef with leaner meats. This includes hot dogs, tacos, and meatloaf, for starters. Turkey is not the devil.

4. Feeling a sense of entitlement to several courses of desserts throughout the day. Most specifically, the nightly slice of cake he enjoys right before bed while I sit there sipping a cup of tea with skim fucking milk. Good times.

5. Responding with seemingly genuine surprise when confronted with the fact that we own a functioning scale. You know, that thing I stand on while yelling every profane phrase I've ever picked up.

6. Having a pre-dinner before we go out for a meal at a restaurant.

7. Ordering General Tso's Chicken. Ever. End of story. Unless your goal is to double your BMI in a month. Then, by all means, have at it, and don't forget that egg roll on the side.

8. Requesting another form of starch as a side to one's pasta dinner.

I think this is a good start for the weight loss beginner and also demonstrates the lengths to which I'm willing to go in the name of dietary schadenfreude.

Before you get too excited in a show of yogurt-loathing solidarity, let me manage your expectations. Having known my husband for fifteen years, it's fair to say that things always tend to work out for him with minimal effort on his part. Sometime in a previous life, he upgraded to the Platinum Karma package.

So, here's my prediction. He'll try it my way for a couple of days, and then he'll decide he doesn't want to suffer like the majority of humans in the history of refined sugars and complex carbohydrates. Then he'll glance at a treadmill out of the corner of his eye, scale back on a few desserts and starches for forty eight hours and drop eight pounds. Done. No big deal.

In his defense, I bet he'll be a total gentleman about it and not tell me he reached his goal weight in the time it took me to write this. Then, he'll offer to make me my tea with skim fucking milk.

And then he'll probably bust out his secret emergency stash of Entenmann's.


*KIM FORDE writes about the art of perfecting domestic failure on her blog, The Fordeville Diaries. A former New York City resident, she is now a secret suburban convert with residual urban road rage. She can often be found in yoga pants and a minivan with her husband, three young kids and pug, managing her Starbucks dependency and healthy fear of craft stores. Kim has written for several humor and parenting blogs, and including* The HuffingtonPost, Scary mommy, *and* Aiming Low, *and was recognized as a 2013 Humor Voice of the Year by BlogHer. She also appeared in the New York City production of Listen to Your Mother, and is a contributor to the anthologies,* I Just Want to Pee Alone *and* "You Have Lipstick on Your Teeth."

*Armed with a keyboard and an addiction to storytelling, she spends more time on blogging and social media than she's prepared to admit.*

# That's Beans, Bitch!
## By Lisa Newlin
### *Lisa Newlin ... Seriously?*

I'm a liar; so much so that my pants might actually be on fire.

I realize you have no reason to believe this assertion as I've just told you I'm a liar, so I could very easily be lying about lying. However, I'm not bright enough to peel through the layers of lying about lying. I also don't have the energy, so please believe that this tale of deceit is most certainly true.

The story begins with my husband and his "selective" taste in foods. He's a picky eater whose favorite foods are on par with that of a toddler. Forget filet mignon; he'd rather have filet o' fish. Steak tartare? He'd prefer Steak Ums with tartar sauce.

Needless to say, cooking for a man with such a delicate palate can be challenging and every once in a while I like to make something that isn't served with a glass of milk and a side of applesauce. This can be difficult with a husband with such discriminating taste buds. Difficult, but not impossible, if you're willing to lie. Which I am.

During the winter months I love to make soups and one of my favorites is taco soup. It has all of the basic food groups in one bowl; meat, veggies, beans, and Fritos. It's perfection. I've been warming bodies and cleaning colons with this recipe for years. However, when I met my husband he advised he didn't like beans, so he couldn't eat taco soup. This was not the response I hoped for.

I decided to make it for him anyway. The first time I did I debated whether to add beans. I knew he wouldn't eat it if I did, but I also knew the beans were what gave it the strong flavor. I decided the only way to maintain the integrity of the soup was to sacrifice mine. I lied to him about the ingredients.

Because my husband is not only picky but also observant, I knew I couldn't just dump the beans into the soup undetected. Rather, I had to go incognito. For that, I implored the use of the food processor, who was happy to accommodate after sitting in the cabinet untouched for years.

I dumped the cans of beans in the processor and pureed them into a paste. I then dumped the paste into the taco soup mixture, returning the food processor to the cabinet where it would sit untouched for another six months.

When it came time to eat, I dished out a heaping bowl of soup and handed it to my husband. We sat down to eat and I anxiously awaited his verdict, knowing he was eating a heaping bowl of deceit.

"This is delicious. What's in it?" he asked, in between mouthfuls of soup.

"It's just a mixture of taco ingredients," I innocently replied, focusing on the layer of Fritos covering my bowl.

"Whatever it is, it's amazing," he responded, quickly devouring each bite.

At that moment I wanted nothing more than to slap the spoon out of his hand and yell, "That's beans, bitch!"

However, I refrained because I'm classy (and because I didn't want to clean up the mess).

I continued that lie for years and all was well until one day it came crashing down like the stacked cans of beans in my cabinet.

One night I was in the kitchen slaving away making taco soup, working up a sweat opening all those cans and dumping them into a pot. I encouraged my husband to lay down in the other room while I made dinner. This was done mostly so he wouldn't see me pureeing beans in the kitchen, but also because I wanted to guilt him into cleaning up the mess after dinner. Allowing him a break was my ticket to martyrdom.

As I dumped the last can of beans into the food processor I heard a squeal. At first I thought it was the neighbor kids, but then I realized the sound was coming from *inside the house*.

I looked up to find my husband standing in the doorway with a look of horror on his face.

"Ew!" He yelled out like an eight year old who just learned where babies come from. "I'm not eating that now."

And that's when I lost it. All those years of hiding the cans of beans, pureeing them to perfection and serving them in secret all came out in one strong "No."

Fortunately, I was able to follow up with more.

"You *will* eat it, and you *will* like it," I admonished. "I've been making it this way for years and you've never complained. You actually like it. Do you know what makes this dinner so delicious?!" I asked.

"No," he mumbled quietly as he dug his big toe into a groove in the floor.

"It's beans, bitch!" I yelled emphatically, slamming the wooden ladle on the counter for effect. "Do you know how many steps I've taken over the years to hide this from you? From the grocery store to the recycling bin, it's been a web of deceit and it's going to continue. You're going to go in the other room and wait for dinner to be served and pretend like this never happened. Pay no attention to the man behind the curtain; or in this case, the woman behind the food processor."

The look in my eyes told him I was a breath away from making a shiv out of the can of beans, and the tone of my voice told him I would use it. He backed away slowly and returned to the TV where he sat quietly until dinner.

I thought I heard whimpering at one point, but I can't be certain.

We had a nice dinner and the soup was superb. He didn't say much, but at the end he mustered up the courage to ask one question.

"That bean-less chili you make? Does that have beans in it too?" His voice was shaky and inquisitive, but there was a fear in his face that told me he didn't want to know the answer.

I thought about how to respond and figured there was no reason to burst his culinary bubble.

"Of course that chili is bean-less," I responded in my sweetest voice. "After all, you don't like beans."

How could I tell him that his favorite "bean-less" chili had three different kinds of beans in it? Would I also have to tell him that his favorite stuffed chicken breasts are made with the cream cheese he so despised? I just couldn't open that can of worms ... or that can of beans.

What damage would the ongoing white lies do anyway? Probably nothing. After all, aren't all good marriages based on a strong foundation of lies and fear? Isn't that the recipe for a long and happy relationship? It certainly is in my cookbook.

Interestingly, it's also a recipe that sometimes calls for beans. Pureed, of course.

*LISA NEWLIN is a humor blogger who plays an unconvincing lawyer in real life. She shouldn't be allowed around sharp objects, anything breakable, or anything with carbohydrates. She prefers dogs over most people, and food over most everything. Her blog, Lisa Newlin ... Seriously?, will make you feel better about your own life. It will also remind you that vodka is the answer to everything, except if the question is "What should I throw on this fire?" Then the answer is definitely NOT vodka.*

# I Just Want to Sleep Alone
## By Abby Heugel
### Abby Has Issues

It was when he reached down into the console of his truck, picked out a used golf tee and started using it as a toothpick that I decided I was done—not just with that date, but with dating in general.

This particular guy was probably the fourth or fifth I had gone out with since getting out of a six-year relationship, one that looking back probably should have been a clue.

It's not that Long Relationship was a bad guy—as I'm sure Toothpick Boy wasn't either for some other germ-loving gal who doesn't mind using dirty sports props to pick lettuce out of a molar—but I learned that certain things are required in order for me to maintain my questionable levels of sanity.

And even though it means that waking up with hummus in my hair is the closest to breakfast in bed that I get, one of those things is I just want to sleep alone.

**Survival Instinct**

I should preface the rest of this by saying that my current level of commitment extends to the Ziploc bag I frugally rinse and reuse for a week at a time and a fake tree I once tried to water. Once Long Relationship and a few rebound Romeos were out of the picture, it was like a light bulb went off.

I was about twenty one at the time and I spent that summer sowing wild oats. (*And by that I mean waking up hung-over in a frat house and frantically searching for my bra before eventually finding it stuck in a ceiling fan.*)

There were questionable decisions (*see above*) and a few bumps on the road to independence, but along with discovering my lack of tolerance for both alcohol and frat boys, I discovered one glorious thing—the fact that I had the whole damn bed to myself.

Sure, getting tangled up in another person can be fun and emotionally fulfilling and all that stuff portrayed in romantic comedies, but it can also be as annoying and uncomfortable as listening to someone clip their toenails. (*Another thing that I don't deal with.*)

There were countless times when a heavy arm or leg would be thrown over me as my bedmate tried to nuzzle up in some semblance of semi-conscious, suffocating spooning. When done correctly, I admit gentle snuggling can be nice...*for a maximum of 2.3 seconds*. After that, any additional limbs that are covering my own as I try and slip into slumber are subject to forceful removal.

Why, you ask?

Because after that amount of time my own arms and legs often go numb, the circulation cut off from the weight of those hairy man limbs haphazardly placed on my own. It then becomes much less about cuddling and more about basic survival.

If your bedmate simply can't take a hint—*and by "hint," I mean shouting, "GET OFF ME YOU HEATHEN!" or "accidentally" placing a pillow gently over his face* —that "embrace" can feel like a bear trap that captures your comfort, your hopes and *(literally)* your dreams.

But in the interest of being proactive, I'll share a tip. If caught in that situation multiple times, a quick solution is to sacrifice podiatry perfection and keep those feet as rough as sandpaper, those nails as sharp as talons. One swipe of the foot or jab with the nail as you fake a leg spasm should help secure some space, at which point in time you are free to drift off again.

**Silence is Golden**

Which brings me back to my point that sleeping alone brings you freedom in various forms.

When you sleep alone you can starfish the sheets all through the night, flail your arms, bounce, twist from side to back to stomach, monopolize the blanket, turn the fan directly on your face, turn the fan away from your face ten minutes later, get up to pee six times a night and no one is going to say a damn word about it.

In fact, no one is going to say a word, period.

There will be no one snoring, hogging the sheets *(except for you,)* asking you to turn off the light, farting *(except for you)* or picking up of the phone to talk to his mom at one in the morning because her bird is humping the plastic circles in his cage and she doesn't know how to make it stop.

# I Just Want to Be Alone

*(Yes, that really happened. It seems that even parrots need a little sexual healing, and this feathered friend's exhibitionist ways were misconstrued by an overprotective human mother as a sign of his imminent demise, and not masturbation. Come to think of it, that might explain a lot about her son.)*

At any rate, while your Cheerio-sized bladder might wake you up too early in the morning, sleeping alone also ensures you will never be prodded from slumber with the little, "poke, poke, poke" of an "early rising" anatomical member from a bedmate and the morning breath that accompanies it.

There is a time and place for this gesture, of course, but it's not when you want to sleep in. Aggressive attempts may even have you considering the installation of plastic circles of your own for him so you can finally drift off again.

## Revealing Victoria's Secret

Finally, I would be remiss if I didn't talk about the benefits of solo sleeping in terms of attire.

Now I'm not "girly-girly" at all—the description of my wardrobe and beauty regime can be summed up with "comfort" and "if I have to"—but I understand that one is expected to own at least a couple pairs of underwear that are a bit sexier than a six-pack of Hanes from Target.

Even if you're a swinging single and no one ever sees the contents of it in action, a little extra color or some leopard print design might be just what you need to get your proverbial panties out of a bunch some days. And I would be lying if I said I've never strutted across the kitchen in heels and a fun little number while pushing a vacuum and singing Beyoncé.

But let's be practical, people.

No one wants to sleep in that stuff.

I believe most men enjoy the pregame show, but they couldn't care less if you're wearing a Victoria's Secret four-color, invisible line lacy bikini bottom with magic unicorn dust or a burlap bag bedazzled with Puff Paint and scented magic markers once the game starts, so to speak, and especially after the final touch down.

But unfortunately, you rarely see Victoria's Secret commercials or movies portraying the gorgeous woman curling up in bed with granny panties, socks in the winter and an old sweatshirt with multiple wine stains.

Now perhaps you're some sex maven that can do a triple back flip off your sex swing with perfect form, and wearing a forty five dollar thong is necessary to complete your performance before romancing your Romeo and then falling into a sexy slumber for the night. In that case, more panty power to you.

*(But even then, you could still kindly ask him to sleep on the spare bed or couch.)*

However, for the majority of us who have retired the sex swing in favor of a Papasan chair, sleeping in fancy underwear just doesn't make that much sense most of the time.

Plus, for the cost of one pair of those fancy drawers, you can purchase a dozen that you won't have to try and discreetly pull out of your crotch or only wear once because you don't know how to wash it without it disintegrating in the machine.

I would consider that a total win-win.

There are those who enjoy sharing a bed, and like I mentioned, I can see how it has an appeal—a warm body on a cold night, someone to bring you some water or hear all about the completely ordinary but fascinating dream you just had.

But for some of us, it took a golf tee, a horny parrot, numb limbs and the freedom to hog all the sheets to realize the true Victoria's Secret—I just want to sleep alone.

# I Just Want to Be Alone

*ABBY HEUGEL is a professional writer and editor of national trade publications for employment, but an award-winning humor blogger and writer at <u>AbbyHasIssues.com</u> for enjoyment.*

*Among other accolades, her work has been featured on* The Huffington Post *and Erma Bombeck Writers' Workshop and she has self-published two books filled with her award-winning humor essays. With a tagline of "I run mental marathons in yoga pants and document my brilliant insights," Abby reminds us that she has issues, but we all do.*

# Dear Magnolia, Should I Marry This Man?
## By Magnolia Ripkin
### *Magnolia Ripkin*

If you have a history of bad boyfriends, possess terrible instincts, and have committed a laundry list of questionable decisions, you have come to the right place.

As an advice writer, it is my job to make sure you get the straight goods before you screw up something important. There are few things more significant than picking your life mate.

Women write to me constantly to ask if they should take the leap and marry their loves. They are unsure about the big issues: Will he stop playing Grand Theft Auto, and/or ever learn to pick up his socks from the damned floor? These are good questions, kittens, truly. This is the sort of momentous stuff you need to know for future domestic partnerships, and blunt advice will be rolled out here in a series of wild generalizations and sharp reproofs. You don't think I write this shit sober, do you?

Fifty percent of people in relationships are wrong for each other. The divorce statistics of the last twenty years are filled with sad sack stories of crappy marriages, but, when you look closely, there are usually two culprits to blame for the broken relationships:

1. Dudes who don't want to grow up.
2. Women who think the wedding day is the most stressful part of the marriage.

The fact that most people are pretty clueless about how to run a relationship is not going to help the situation. Learning-by-doing is all fun and games until somebody loses an eye. Incidentally, there should be a licensing bureau where testing is done to see if you are too stupid to marry or reproduce. When I am running the world, we will totally have that.

Picking a life partner is no easy task. Hell, simply finding a guy who isn't a compulsive finger-sniffer is hard enough. Getting the personality mix right takes effort. Oh, and for the record, ladies, he isn't always the problem in the relationship. Some of you girls are bat-shit crazy, and when he gets one look at your twelve cats and gift wrapping room with seventy three boxes of craft supplies, a smart lad will run away – screaming.

I am going to assume you found somebody, and he doesn't have big red flags sticking out of his forehead. This means he doesn't have baby Mamas across three states, or worse, live in his Mom's basement, confused at the prospect of running the washing machine. Scratch the surface and see what he is hiding. If your friends and family have already expressed doubts about this guy, you should listen to them. Seriously, if you don't heed their warning, they will buy out the entire "I-Told-You-So" section of the card store for your divorce party.

Let's assume this man you have found is actual "future husband" material. He has popped the question and likely given you a substandard diamond (because his buddies helped him pick it out). If you helped him choose the ring, at least he knows you are going to be a control freak, so extra points to you for transparency. You have decided to make a life together; now it all starts for real.

Picking a particular dude to marry is kind of like BASE jumping for the first time. You've checked your parachute, you have tested the ropes and safety gear, but stepping off the ledge still makes you fill your shorts. Or it should. If you aren't at least a little bit nervous, you clearly don't understand the situation. Spend an afternoon in family court and see what happens when it falls apart. That might be you someday shrieking across the judge's bench while your four hundred dollar an hour lawyer watches you hurl obscenities at your ex and his twenty-three-year-old pregnant girlfriend. That is what "happily ever after" means sometimes.

I believe that advice from the school of hard knocks is the best kind. I won't put sparkles on it for you, so sit down and listen up. In order to prepare for your life with a man, you need to fully grasp that you are the owner and proprietor of the six square inches of real estate he cares about most. No matter what he says, men only pick a partner so they can stop being rejected in bars. What they don't understand is that they now wear a leash disguised as their pretty new wife. Don't worry, they like the leash and will follow along happily most of the time. One proviso: you must try not to use sex as currency. Just make him aware that the girl parts are only available when their life support system is pleased. *Capiche?*

The next big important lesson is the same advice I give about parenting and dog training: *Begin as you mean to proceed*. As an illustration, imagine you get a cute little puppy. You let him up on the couch whenever he pleases because he is so darned adorable. Then Bowser hits sixty pounds, rolls in mud, farts, and licks himself when you have company. Now you try to train him to stay on the floor, and he has no idea why you don't want him up on your lap anymore. He will resent being on the floor and retaliate by chewing the crotch out of your underwear. If you had started with the floor-only rule, he might learn to put the fricken' toilet seat down – ahem … we are talking about the dog, right? Sorry.

Man can be a primitive creature. When you first set up domestic residence, you must ensure that he has his own "cave." As soon as you have kids you can convert it to a play room. You will always be able to say "I tried to give you your own space but the babies needed it." Speaking of caves, when you have gone all Mama Bear on his ass about something, give him some space and time alone to come to his own conclusion about how totally wrong he was.

Then there is the mother-in-law thing. It is absolutely a fact that he will favor his Mother over you in a conflict situation. These brouhahas will swirl around particular issues such as children, Christmas, and how ineptly you make his special foods. She had him first, but you have him now. This is a dicey negotiation, and I wish I could tell you it is helpful to make her watch while you pee on his leg, but sadly it doesn't work. She won't concede that you own his ass now. I suggest the direct approach. Look your man in the eye and tell him that he has to take your side when his mother gets in his face about you. The correct tool for this conversation is a cattle prod, the electric kind. (Avon used to sell them, I am sure.)

When you first got this man, he likely came with some buddies he has kept around since primary school. You have about two years in the beginning of your life together to selectively assassinate his most disruptive bromances. If you leave it too long, you will never get rid of "that friend" you hate. Like sleeve snot, that male pal just won't go away on his own, so you must handle it with surgical precision. Don't be obvious about it or your man will just hold on tighter. Be subtle, and over time he will forget his precious and move on. He will occasionally wax poetic about all the fun they had and the memories they shared. When he begins to reminisce, touch his penis in that special way and he will remember where he is meant to be.

Finances are a dangerous and sensitive topic for couples. Negotiating this is like trying to claw your way through blackberry bushes – naked – while acid rains on you, searing your open wounds. It gets really strained if one of you decides to stay home and has no income. The tsunami of power imbalance will screw your shit up. Negotiate the terms as early as possible. Then, the second your offspring are in school, get some sort of income. Hang around a divorce lawyer for a day and see what happens to people who have no earning power of their own and out-of-date skill sets. Get used to eating cat food.

The topic of children is one that often comes across my desk from people seeking advice. Women are either whining about wanting more of them or complaining about their husband trying to plant another sprite into their lady vault. Normally one would have agreed on this sort of thing ahead of time. I suggest this: have your first one. If it is ugly, don't have another one. If you get a cute one, then you can safely consider making another. Easy.

And this brings me to the bedroom. Well, technically it brings *you* to the bedroom. If either of you have been hiding your freak flag, the time to bring out the tickle-trunk of leather masks and whips should probably be sometime before the engagement. If you can hardly wait to get your partner into that special chair with chains you bought at the "nasty dirty store," you will want to have that conversation before you give it to him as a wedding gift. Even if you aren't kinky kangaroos, have lots of sex anyway; it keeps him happy and you from being a shrieking unfulfilled bitch. If he isn't any good at it … teach him. Use your words or I have heard diagrams work really well. If he is still being dense, use Ken and Barbie to demonstrate how the parts fit together.

Also, another pretty key thing to agree upon is precisely what constitutes "cheating." I know, you are thinking "Everybody knows what cheating means!" Not so. Sometimes they think there is a gray area. You see, big boys like having their pee pees touched, so just make it clear that the only people who can handle his gear are you, and his urologist. That's it. Yes, sexting counts as being disloyal. There is no better way of making this clear than to make him take his cell phone to the hospital … in his arse … to have it removed.

It might surprise you that sometimes opposites marry. I know, crazy, right? When one of you is social and the other is a hermit, you will never ever agree on parties, dinners, social events or travel plans. In some marriages the "he and she" cannot agree on one single thing when it comes to their social life. These marriages tend to last because the talker sometimes fills the empty space when the other runs out of intelligent things to say. Or the quiet one goes deaf, which works too. It is a well-documented fact that the talky one in the relationship can actually bust a hemorrhoid from the strain of shutting their pie hole, so they are better matched with the quiet type.

On the topic of opposites, there is a pretty good chance one of you has a metabolism delivered by unicorns to the mother's womb in a magic conch shell, granting lifelong thinness. The other (let's face it, it's probably you, honey) got your fat cell storage capacity from Satan. There is nothing that kills a game of hide-the-salami faster than when he pinches your inch and says, "I see the pudge fairy has left an offering on your ass." If he does that, give him no sex. Simple. Even the most unevolved single-celled amoebas can learn to stay away from danger. Surely he is capable of figuring out that the more self-conscious you feel, the less naked you will ever be. One of my friends has a husband who makes it his personal mission to keep her fit and slim. When he goes out of town, she shame-eats pizza. I suggested she shame-fuck the pool boy instead – that marriage isn't going to last.

Finally, if you think he is going to be all you ever need, then you are either nineteen or you are stupid. He should be your best friend, and your marriage should be a sacred place, but you have to have a life outside it. Your women friends will hold your hair when you barf into the toilet and they will likely outlive your husband. They will also stand by you so pick the ones that would help you hide his body. Those girls should be your bitch posse.

We all figure out how to work with our partners over time. The more shrieking you do, and the more avoidance he practices, the harder it will be to get to a happy place. Negotiate stuff clearly ahead of time. Men love clarity and simple instructions. Oh, and if you are using the word "fine" as a weapon, then you are being an emotionally immature little girl.

In case you missed the point, ALWAYS have a way to make money that doesn't involve him, and for shit's sake, have interests that don't see you following him around like a little dog. Keep your own dignity, your own rights, and don't ever wash his car ... ever.

I bet your Mom has told you some of this stuff, but now you have it direct from "She-who-is-always-right" as well.

And finally, grow some chick balls and love the hell out of the boy you picked. If he is worth anything, he will deserve it.

*MAGNOLIA RIPKIN is like that mouthy opinionated Aunt you always regret inviting to family dinners. She drinks too much then tells you how to run your life. Although she is usually right, it feels like you just got a glass of cold water in the face.*

*Channeling Erma Bombeck and Dear Abby, this matriarch is flinging out blunt advice on her blog, answering pressing questions about business, personal development, parenting, heck even the bedroom isn't safe. Her writing is sometimes a guide to fixing your life, and other times it is just full on fiction to make you laugh. Just don't make her angry.*

*She can be found expounding excitedly on her diverse views through her blog magnoliaripkin.com. She is also the Editor in Chief over at bluntmoms.com and a regular contributor to Huffington Post.*

# True Love Story
## By A.K. Turner
### *A.K. Turner*

"Go ahead, you two," my mother urged. "Try it out."

I stood with my mother and Mike in the middle of a mattress store. There was so much I still didn't know about him, yet there we were bed shopping. The three of us hovered over a cheaper model, and my mother encouraged us to test it, this mass of springs and fabric that touted spinal health and promised not to go up in flames, at least not quickly, should a fire break out.

Shopping with my mother and boyfriend for a mattress was not a situation I'd ever anticipated. Mike and I looked at the pristine, white rectangle with its faint paisley imprint and felt a collective shame for all that would eventually take place on this bed. Despite my mother's encouragement, the feeling remained—that awkward, giddy embarrassment of blushes that accompany such a purchase in the presence of a parent. We had every intention of living in sin.

I was twenty-one, Mike was twenty, and my mother had met him twelve hours earlier. I was thankful for her blessing, evidenced by her support of mattress-testing, despite the fact that she hardly knew him. He was young and strong and good-looking, but almost too much so, the kind of good-looking that makes you anticipate a person will be an asshole. He had the muscled arms and perfect bone structure of a handsome-but-jerky captain of the football team from an after-school special, and I secretly harbored the fear that he hid a gross defect of character. What if he tortured small animals or had affairs with men in gas stations or was the type of guy who peed all over the toilet seat? I was already in love with him, so there was no turning back. But I really hoped he wouldn't pee all over the toilet seat.

I'd met him three months earlier on a ten-day vacation in Mexico, where we were free from the responsibilities of work and school and U.S. laws on public drunkenness. Meeting someone on vacation tends to speed up the dating process. Instead of meeting once a week for dinner or a movie, you eat all your meals together and wake up together, looking at each other with mirrored expressions of confusion and tentative utterances of "Did we …"

Mike was vacationing with his family, and on more than one morning of our ten days in Mexico, I'd had to exit his room and pass through the condo kitchen with my eyes on the floor, under the scrutiny of his mother as she made coffee. Sixteen years later, she still relishes telling the stories of my walks of shame.

When the vacation ended, we said goodbye in the airport. Without warning, my emotions rudely took control of my body and reduced me to a puddle of snot and tears, which was certainly not what I wanted as Mike's last image of me. His parents were there that day, and as Mike boarded his plane, I cried on his mother's shoulder while his father, completely befuddled as to how to handle such a situation, feigned sudden enthrallment with a Mexican soap opera on a nearby monitor.

We spent three months pining and hundreds of dollars on phone bills before I decided to pack up my electric-blue Volkswagen Rabbit and travel from Maryland to California to be with him. He was in his first year of college. I was in my last. We agreed that if one of us were going to move, it would be me.

"*How* long were you two in Mexico together?" my mother asked when I told her I was moving.

"Ten days."

"And you want to drive across the country and move in with him?"

"Yes," I confirmed.

I knew that my family might think my decision indicated insanity, drugs, or pregnancy. I held my breath for my mother's reaction.

"Okay," she said. "Want me to drive with you?"

Two weeks later, I pulled up to her house and loaded her tiny suitcase, all that I would permit her, into my packed Volkswagen. She held a newspaper in hand as she opened the passenger side door.

"What's that?" I questioned, motioning to the newspaper.

"What's what?"

"In your hand," I demanded.

"It's a newspaper."

"Yeah, you can't bring that."

"What are you talking about?" She looked confused.

"Sorry, there's just no room."

"No room for my newspaper?"

"You'll have to leave that here."

"I'll just keep it on my lap," she protested.

"You can't," I explained. "I already have your lap items designated."

Lucky for me, my mother was a sport, and after three thousand forty-seven miles and days spent surviving on gas-station food, we arrived in a tiny, coastal California town.

"Should we pick up a pizza?" I asked.

"Don't you want to go straight there to see him?" my mother questioned. "You're not getting cold feet, are you?"

"No," I answered. "He's at a crew competition in some other town. He won't be back until tomorrow."

"In that case," she said, "I'd rather find a liquor store."

"Jackpot." I pulled into a strip mall that offered both Little Caesars and liquor. After the week of Pringles and Diet Coke, it felt like fine dining.

"I'll buy these," my mother said in the liquor store, holding up one each of the largest available bottles of gin and vodka. "Consider it a housewarming present."

"Aw, thanks, Mom."

We pulled into the apartment complex long after dark but well before midnight. Balancing pizza and booze, we left the car packed with my possessions and went searching in the dark for the apartment number Mike had given me. I felt a bit like a prowler, but carrying booze made it seem like I was a prowler bearing gifts, which wasn't quite so creepy.

Standing outside the apartment door in California, I knocked because that's what doors ask of me. I followed this with a kick at the doormat where he'd agreed to hide a key. The doormat slid to the side easily, revealing no key underneath. For a brief but heavy moment, I wondered if I was the victim of the most elaborate and cruel prank ever conceived. Get a girl to fall for you, so much so that she quits her job, gives up her apartment, leaves the state during her last semester of college, and drags her mother across the country to meet Mr. Wonderful, who really lives somewhere else entirely and engages in this sadism because he gets off on it. *Fucker.*

But then the door opened.

Mike stood before us, eyes narrowed with sleep and standing in only his boxer shorts. I wondered what my mother would think. Would she purse her lips in disapproval? What if part of his package was hanging out and he didn't know it? *Please let his penis be in place*, I thought. I checked, and all seemed tidily confined, no errant testicle peeking out from bunched-up boxers. I looked to my mother for her reaction. She beamed.

"Hi," said Mike, looking stunned but pleased. "I thought you wouldn't be here until tomorrow."

"And I thought you were on a crew trip."

"Come in," he said and stepped back.

We entered the apartment, suddenly full of awkward tension. My mother and I headed straight for the kitchen to set down the pizza and booze.

"Mom," I said, "this is Mike. Mike, this is my mother, Edie."

"Hi, Edie." He smiled.

"Hi, Mike." She continued to beam.

"Maybe you should go put some clothes on," I suggested, embarrassed that the full hotness of the man I was moving in with was right there on display for his first meeting with my mom.

"He's fine," she chided. "Leave him alone."

"Oh, sorry, I'll be right back," said Mike, ducking out of the kitchen to search for clothes.

As soon as he was out of earshot, my mom turned into a teenager. "Oh my God, he's *so* cute. Did you see the way he *looked* at you?" Then, in a lower voice, "What am I doing here? This should be your moment. I feel like an *intruder*."

We unpacked the Volkswagen of my random assortment of

possessions that seemed worthless, but managed to occupy the entire vehicle. Clothes, silverware, toiletries, a framed poster of Billie Holiday, a hammer, a lamp. I'd had my books shipped ahead of time. Just as his athletic activities seemed alien to me, for I'd never before known someone who rowed on a crew team, so did my attachment to books to him.

We had a drink, pizza, and attempted to relax. And then it was time to go to bed, which was ironically anything but relaxing. We had no beds. Mike's furniture consisted of a lone bookshelf. He'd moved into the apartment from a dorm room, just in time for my arrival. The bookshelf, combined with my lamp, hammer, poster, and spoons, did little to flesh out the place. He had two thin camping pads. We gave the thicker of the two to my mother and took the remaining camping pad and placed it on the carpet in the middle of a bare bedroom. We slept in a prolonged hug while clothed, the sleep of two people who love but hardly know each other, in a room just a wall away from my mother.

The next morning, the three of us set out on a shopping trip. We bought pots and pans at Goodwill, and I couldn't help but wonder about the undoubtedly dead people whose cookware I was inheriting for a dollar thirty-five apiece. *Hopefully none of them died of Teflon poisoning,* I thought.

At Target we picked out bedding and random objects like a trashcan for the bathroom. I eyed a scale and debated buying it. A woman walked by and said, "Honey, don't do that to yourself." I returned the scale to its shelf.

We went to a mattress store because I didn't think I could take another night pretending that a camping pad on carpet was comfortable, and because we were now the proud new owners of bedding, but no bed to put it on. My mom would be forced to tough it out on the camping pad for two more nights before flying back to the East Coast.

Buying     a     mattress     with     your     brand-new,     I-hardly-know-you-and-really-hope-this-works-out,     wait-what-the-fuck-are-we-doing significant other is … awkward. Throwing my mother into the mix did nothing to lessen the discomfort of the situation.

"Go ahead, you two," she said, motioning to the low-end queen. "Try it out."

Mike and I looked at each other and then tentatively laid down on the mattress, a prudish foot of space between us, both of us stock straight with arms tucked in tight at our sides. The fluorescent lights of the mattress store seemed to highlight the reality of our moving in together. My mother stood off to the side, smiling in an ill-fated attempt to put us at ease.

She turned away from us, pretending to be interested in a nearby pillow-top, which gave me the sudden urge to run and hug her. Instead, I lay still, feeling the energy of lying next to a man on a mattress *we* would buy *together*. While staring at the ceiling, and without a word, our hands met in the space between us.

"This could work," he said.

I wasn't sure if he meant the mattress or us. Either way, I agreed. "Let's try it out."

"Wait," he whispered. "*Here?*"

*A.K. TURNER is the author of* This Little Piggy Went to the Liquor Store, Mommy Had a Little Flask, *and* Hair of the Corn Dog, *as well as a coauthor of* Drinking with Dead Women Writers *and* Drinking with Dead Drunks *with Elaine Ambrose. She is a former radio host and writer-in-residence for the city of Boise, and she frequently speaks at conferences, writing retreats, and comedy events. After seventeen years and two mattress upgrades, she and Mike now live with their two daughters in Idaho. Harass her at* AKTurner.com.

# The Unwritten Rules of a (Mostly) Happy Marriage
## By Courtney Fitzgerald
### *Our Small Moments*

I should have known our married life would be FULL of interesting stories, starting with our wedding reception. We are the only couple, I have ever known, who did not even get one little morsel of their wedding cake. (We forgot to feed each other, and we didn't even think to save the top. That's what you get for hiring a cheap wedding photographer. Stupid kids.)

On our second day of marriage, Scott lost his keys to our car and our apartment. After an interesting scavenger hunt that lasted a couple of hours, we found our keys. We were only slightly late to our present opening, and we quickly learned how to break into our apartment. At that point, we had been married for less than twenty-four hours and already had a few good stories of misadventures, as well as valuable marriage lessons.

However, nothing prepared us for the learning experience known as THE FIRST YEAR OF MARRIAGE. These lessons go beyond, "Never go to sleep angry," and I'm sure the reason why we stayed happily married is because we FOLLOWED these rules every day, well the good days anyway.

### Rule #1: We should NEVER, EVER cook together.

Since we did not live together before marriage, one of us always cooked for the other, or more importantly, we ate out. Scott cooked for both of us most of the time. He was a sous chef and I was clearly not allowed in a professional kitchen. However, once we were married, we were grownups and married grownups cook and eat at home, or so we thought. Our first and only cooking together experience, we decided to make an enchilada recipe from our new cookbook. It started out fine, as we gathered the ingredients and utensils together. However, it turned unbelievably UGLY when I tried to deviate from the recipe.

"Um, Courtney, what ARE you doing?"

"I am adding a touch of garlic to the recipe. I've seen this before."

"No, that's not what it says. We need to follow the directions so it turns out OK."

"Well, in other recipes, they use garlic, so I am adding just a touch."

"But this recipe does NOT call for garlic. Good cooks follow the directions. Someone else already tested it, so we need to do what it says," my new husband insisted. That's when the scene moved from a heated discussion to a real argument, or at least a really dumb argument.

"Well, that's stupid reasoning. Why not TRY something new?"

"Maybe this is why you are NOT a GOOD cook? Did you ever think of that? Maybe, if you followed the recipe, your food would taste better."

"Stop being a jerk! Are we really fighting over garlic??!" I stormed out of the room and slammed the bedroom door.

We never cooked together again. From that day forward, we divided and conquered in the kitchen, the rare occasions we assembled meals together.

**Rule #2: You can, in fact, run out of money.**

Within the first three months of our marriage, I graduated from college, and we moved halfway across the country with wedding money and one clear credit card to our names. We didn't have jobs or a place to live, but those were some small, unimportant details at the time.

A few weeks later, we each had crappy employment, a tiny apartment, and all was well on payday. Every other day of the month, we got creative in order to survive. We learned to walk to a certain Chinese restaurant to share ONE egg roll when we needed to feel air conditioning. We were champs at making that one egg roll last as long as the best 3 course meal. Air conditioning was worth savoring an egg roll. Sometimes, we even had four dollars and eighteen cents for us EACH to have ice cream at our favorite stand, however, most of the time, we had to share, or go to McDonald's for cheap soft serve goodness.

"I NEED ice cream tonight."

"We get paid tomorrow, chew on an ice cube. You could freeze peanut butter." I replied.

"I bet we can find two dollars and nine cents laying around. I REALLY, REALLY want some."

"If you can find it, I will happily share it."

"If you want to share it, then you need to help me find money."

We searched and searched like two dogs who forgot where they hid their bones. We checked in our usual extra change places and eventually found one dollar and ninety-nine cents. So freaking close to our treat, yet so far away.

Giving up, I said, "It's no use, I have looked everywhere. NO ICE CREAM FOR YOU!"

"Did you check the ashtray in the car?"

"Yes."

"Did you check the change bucket."

"It's officially empty."

"Underwear drawer?"

"Yep."

"Couch?"

"Clean, for a change."

"There has to be one dime SOMEWHERE in our house."

Seconds later, Scott was jumping up and down like a crazy person. "I found one! I found one!" He exclaimed, dancing around holding up a dime. "Whoo hoo!"

"Where did you find that dime?"

"Under the dryer, and now, thanks to me, we get ice cream! Score one for the Scottman!" (I wish that last part was embellished, but alas, it's true.)

**Rule #3: Never wash your clothes together, especially if one of you carries a pen and trash in your pockets.**

Honestly, this is one rule we didn't follow completely, and I regretted it EVERY time we ignored it. Scott had the worst habit of collecting pens and trash in his signature cargo pants. Like an idiot, I forgot to check his pockets, and when I actually remembered, either gum or a pen would fall through the cracks. In case you were wondering, one of those things can easily ruin a WHOLE load of laundry, and the two together, definitely ruined every article of clothing in the load.

I'll never forget the first one we ruined. I believe it was two days after buying the only BRAND NEW washer/dryer combo we ever owned.

"Oh, sh- sh- sh-oot!"

"What's wrong?"

"There's ink all over the inside of our dryer! How did that happen?"

"Oh, uh, huh, maybe you had a pen in your pocket," my husband stammered.

"But I never carry pens. Bummer!"

As I unloaded the clothes, I noticed item after item with an ink blotch on it somewhere. Finally, I figured it out.

"Um, Scott, YOU had a pen in your pocket."

"No, I'm sure I cleaned them out," he said guiltily. (He KNEW it was HIS fault.)

"Well, this big splotch of ink from your pocket to your crotch says it all," I said throwing his shorts at him.

From then on, every pen load, and believe me, there were lots of them, he simply said, "I thought I checked. I am sorry. Can I take you shopping tonight?"

**Rule #4: Maps - use them, read them, and do what they say, especially in New York City.**

Our first year of marriage was from the spring of 2002 to the spring of 2003. This was before smart phones, GPS systems, and all of the other fancy gear that gives us directions now. We relied upon paper maps purchased from gas stations and Mapquest (if we had color ink to print), mostly, we spent a lot of time in the car, traveling in the direction we THOUGHT we should go, hoping to eventually find our way. It worked most of the time, and one could argue it worked every time since I'm not still lost somewhere on the East Coast today. However, that strategy failed us when driving through New York City.

We drove down to Virginia to spend the Fourth of July with family. Since we drove, we attached our bikes to the back of our 1997 Hyundai Accent, sporting South Dakota license plates. On our way home, we decided to go through NYC because the route was shorter than going around it. I mean, really, how bad could it be, especially in broad daylight?

It wasn't bad, except for the three hours we spent stopped, in traffic, in our unairconditioned, stick shift car. Finally, we were moving, and traffic was FAST. I seriously closed my eyes, so I didn't have to watch the other cars rip the paint off ours. I SHOULD have been looking at the map more closely, but, hey, live and learn. The lanes were jumbled, and at some point we were forced to exit by way of Jerome Avenue in the Bronx. We tried to find a ramp back on the interstate, but didn't see it, I bet it was lost in the million and one other signs or graffiti that decorated the street corners. Our best reasoning was we should keep driving and we'd eventually find our way back. That works in most places, but NOT New York City.

As we drove, we slowly noticed the buildings were getting more and more run down. As soon as we saw a woman with crazy curly hair, wearing a slip, following her hand, we rolled up the windows, despite the ninety degree heat.

We heard a man yelling "Hey! Hey!" at the top of his lungs, as he chased someone out of a building, and both of us carefully reached over to lock the car doors.

"You think we'll get to keep our bikes?"

"Hmm, I hope so, but I'm guessing someone is going to slash them off the car."

"Well, if no one takes our car, that would be a good thing too."

"Yeah, if we make out of here alive, that would also be a good thing."

We kept driving, hoping our small Accent with two bikes on the back would blend in enough that people would leave us alone. While I am sure it DID NOT blend in with this neighborhood, eventually, we crossed a set of train tracks and found ourselves in the greenest, most beautiful neighborhood in Connecticut we ever saw. We made our way out of the Bronx, intact, believe it or not, back on the right road, and continued our drive.

From that point on, we always made sure to have a map in the car when driving through unknown territory. We have never gone back to Jerome Avenue, and I have no plans to hang there either.

**Rule #5 - Always count appliances before moving into a new place.**

Yep, you read that right.

"Count appliances? What do you mean?" you ask.

Well, Scott and I signed a lease on an "as furnished" apartment that happened to be missing a stove AND refrigerator. At the walk-through, we noticed the old, tiny place didn't have a dishwasher, but we could live with that. Our landlady said we'd have to furnish our own washer and dryer, but that's typical. Everything else looked just fine, so we signed our name on the dotted lines and agreed to move in at the end of the week.

One night, before we moved, I awoke in a cold sweat.

"What's wrong with you?" Scott inquired sleepily.

"Um, I don't think our new place has a stove."

"Oh, I know it did. I mean, all apartments have them."

"Where was it?"

"It was next to the, ah … bet it was near, um, wait, I don't think it had a refrigerator either." Now Scott was starting to believe my fear.

"No, it would HAVE to have a fridge, right?"

Our minds were racing, we were both mentally trying to put it all together. I mean, who rents an apartment without appliances? (Two dumb twenty-three year-old newlyweds, that's who.)

Neither one of us could sleep, so we climbed in our car, in the middle of the night, to see if we could peek in the house to prove ourselves wrong. However, we were right. We rented a place without appliances. Welcome to adulthood!

All in time, we got it straightened out, but it took some wheeling, dealing, tears, and bets. If I remember correctly, we actually owe them one of our children, but luckily we never kept our end of the "our apartment needs a stove and refrigerator deal." We never signed a lease on another place without a stove again. At least the two dumb kids were capable of learning.

In eleven years of marriage, I have a million misadventure stories (and I am NOT exaggerating), and I'm certain the reason why we survived is because we followed the simple rules of our relationship that we learned in our adventurous first year of marriage.

*COURTNEY FITZGERALD is a mom, teacher, photographer, writer, dreamer. She loves to laugh, but her readers love it when she makes them cry. She enjoys writing from her heart about life, kids, having a child with autism, and losing her husband to cancer. She writes about her perfectly imperfect family at <u>oursmallmoments.com</u>. Someday, she plans on figuring out what she wants to be when she grows up. You can follow her on <u>Twitter</u>, <u>Pinterest</u>, <u>Facebook</u>, and <u>Instagram</u>.*

# The Rise and Fall of the Three Commandments
## By Andrea C.
### *The Underachiever's Guide to Being a Domestic Goddess*

At the beginning of every fairy tale romance every couple knows they need their own Rules of Engagement if they want their relationship to last. In the early years, when Mark and I moved in together while planning our wedding, we thought it would be wise to set down some basic guidelines. Nothing too disturbing, but just a few rules to live by in order to co-exist in harmony. Those were the blissfully ignorant early days where we could still be selfish because we were just too young to know any different.

Mark's rules were simple:

**1. Don't throw away my shit.**

Mark was a connoisseur of collectibles - anything from comics to posters, T-shirts and hard to find concert memorabilia, political pins and newspaper clippings. He had a reason for keeping all of these things, and 'twas not mine to judge or understand, but to accept, and strongly resist the urge to toss some of these "rare collectibles" in the trash.

**2. Please do not wear, or allow anyone else to wear, stilettos or spiked heels on the beautiful, soft pine floors that I refinished myself.**

Looking back, this just makes me laugh. Now, we have three cats and three boys that have destroyed our floors with their cleats, claws, and constant roughhousing. We are so past caring it's to the point of hilarity. Our naiveté in our twenties was adorable.

**3. Do not, under any circumstances, dry my clothes in the dryer.**

Well, aren't we particular! Mark should have been happy not to have to launder his clothes anymore. Having a nice Greek girl to do his household chores was enough of a gift not to bark orders! Okay, there was that ONE time that I dried his favorite pair of jeans and didn't tell him. When he put them on, he thought he gained weight and immediately started a rigorous workout routine, only to find a few weeks later that I was the one who shrunk his jeans and not his favorite food. That little debacle was how this rule came to be.

He was meticulous about his clothes back then. (Note- the past tense. Nowadays, Mark is beyond grateful not only for the little Greek laundry sprite, but also for an endless supply of clean clothes flowing in his drawers and closets-hang dried or not.)

My rules were equally simple:

**1. Put the toilet seat DOWN, please and thank you.**

It only took one "accidental bidet" incident for me to call him every name in the book at two o'clock in the morning when I got a surprise butt swirly in the dark. Little did I know when I made this rule that, soon enough I'd have three little boys to guarantee more accidental early morning swirlies for years to come.

**2. Never question the amount of products I have in the shower or that I need the entire bathroom counter space for my beauty products, and do not, under any circumstances, come in the bathroom when the door is closed.**

My modern-day needs are now limited to anti-wrinkle cream, concealer, lip gloss and rubber bands for my hair. As far as a closed bathroom door, that's laughable. When I close the door, it's like a secret invitation for all of my children to immediately need to tell me something of extreme urgency.

**3. Retail therapy is much cheaper than a real therapist. Trust me on this and don't question my shopping habits.**

Between talking to my girlfriends, blogging, and shopping, I have saved us thousands of dollars in therapy sessions by handling my stress issues by myself. Drs. TJ Maxx, Marshalls and J. Crew have done wonders for my problems over the years and I highly recommend this alternative to therapy.

After we discussed and agreed on our *Three Simple Rules to Living Together*. We were having the time of our lives planning the wedding, getting into our own little routine and figuring out each other's quirks. It was so much fun and time flew by those first few months. The honeymoon before *The* Honeymoon.

One day at breakfast we decided it was time for a hot date on the town. We wanted to dress up and go out to celebrate our last days of engagement before the wedding mania started. Back then going out was a big deal. It was all about where you went and what you wore while looking glamorous and feeling fabulous. (Modern-day dates include a twice-a-year outing for dinner and drinks or, actually, only one drink because we are too tired. When it comes to drinking, we are now considered lightweights. We turn into pumpkins after nine thirty, so we tend to wrap it up early. Don't get me wrong, we're the life of the party as long as the party is over by nine!)

That morning, we had a nice chat about our evening to come. Mark gave me a gentle reminder that his favorite pants were in the wash and when the cycle was done, would I please hang them so they would be dry for the evening? *Of course, I can do that, my love.*

After working on the wedding details all morning like it was my job, I felt that I needed some retail therapy (see above) before our night out. A leisurely trip to my favorite upscale consignment store to check out their spring arrivals was on the afternoon agenda. The weather was unseasonably mild and I couldn't wait to show off the legs that I'd been beating mercilessly at the gym in preparation for the upcoming nuptials. As I grabbed my beautiful Gucci purse that I picked up on my consignment shop visit, I was attacked by a horsefly that nearly blinded me as it barreled into my eye. WHAT THE HELL? I did a crazy swatting-type of dance, almost injuring myself to get it the hell away from me. I watched the insect fly through the air like a kamikaze on crack, finally landing on the window. *OH, NO YOU DON'T, YOU LITTLE ...* I quickly looked around the room for the closest magazine I could find and noticed one in a box of Mark's things on his desk. I grabbed it immediately and rolled it up as tightly as I could to make a homemade nun chuck type of weapon and smacked the guts right out of that fly, smearing its innards all over the reading material. I tossed the paper nun-chuck onto the couch, grabbed a paper towel, cleaned the window, and, finally departed for my shopping spree.

A few hours and several lattes later, I returned home in a frenzy, knowing I didn't leave myself much time to get glammed up for our date. As I walked into the bathroom, I realized that I had never hung Mark's pants to dry. *Mother ...* ! He only asked me to do one thing today and I forgot. I glanced around as if someone might be watching me, grabbed the pants out of the washer, and tossed them into the dryer. REBEL. RULEBREAKER. REVOLUTIONARY. Yep, that was me. Oh come on, what was the harm in dryer drying them for a few minutes just to get the dampness out? No harm. After I flung them in the dryer, I quickly folded his other t-shirts that had been hanging from the clothesline to make room for his pants after a few twirls in the dryer. I placed them like neat little soldiers in the laundry basket near the machine and went on my way.

I took a quick shower, finished my hair and makeup without incident, and tried on my new outfit that went beautifully with my gorgeous five-inch, BCBG, double-ankle-strap, buckle stilettos, my new found-treasures from a recent retail therapy session at the consignment shop. I couldn't yet tell how the ensemble really looked because I wasn't wearing the shoes. Oh, what the hell! Maybe I'd just slip these on quickly to make sure they looked nice with the clothes. Only it wasn't quick due to the straps with the tiny holes to poke through each buckle. I struggled to get both shoes on and immediately felt glamorous glee as I grew several inches taller. I was jarred out of my daydream by a car door and quickly ran to the window in my heels. *SHIT! SHIT! SHIT! HE'S HOME EARLY! OH MY GOD, HIS JEAAAAAANS!* I ran as fast as I could in five inch heels into the bathroom and flung the door closed behind me, not wanting to get busted in stilettos while the dryer was drying his pants. I was en-route to the dryer when I tripped over the decorative bath mat and flew through the air. Mid-fall I grabbed the towel bar, hoping for a miracle save in the air, but I yanked it right off the wall, sending me and the bar to the ground in one fell swoop. As I hit the ground, the towel bar smashed me in the face, causing my nose to bleed profusely. Luckily, I landed right next to the dryer, so I reached up and opened the dryer door as fast as I could, sheer will urging me to get those jeans out of there. Mark knocked on the bathroom door. "Honey, are you okay in there?"

"JUST A MINUTE," I yelled while swallowing blood. I got the pants half-way out of the dryer when I noticed I was bleeding everywhere. Of course, I didn't want to ruin my beautiful new outfit, so I extended my reach as far as I could to the laundry basket and grabbed the first shirt I felt to cover my face and sop up the blood.

"Honey, you're scaring me, I'm coming in."

"NOOOOOOOO," I yelled in slow motion. But it was too late. He walked in to find me sprawled across the floor, sporting stilettos in the house, drying his jeans in the dryer, and nursing my nose with his beloved Triumph Motorcycle collectible T-shirt that he'd had as long as he could remember.

I was doomed.

He rushed over to me, glancing over at the missing towel rack and darting his eyes between my bloody face and his pants hanging out of the dryer. "For the love of ... Andrea, what the hell happened?"

I came clean and told him exactly what happened. We laughed hysterically and then he said, "Who cares about those stupid rules? You're just lucky you didn't break your nose, chip a tooth, or impale yourself with the towel bar! I love you and that's all that matters. I'll find another pair of pants to wear tonight. Now let's get you cleaned up and get you one of those girly drinks you love so much." He helped me up and walked me over to the couch. As he gently sat me down, he spotted the rolled-up nun chuck.

"OH MY GOD! WHAT DID YOU DO TO MY AMAZING SPIDERMAN NUMBER 129?" he cried picking it up. "I killed a fly with it?" I know it wasn't a question, but I worded it that way, hoping for mercy.

He exhaled, exasperated and at a complete loss for words.

"I must really love you, you know that? That comic book was worth about three hundred bucks. I was going to take that box of comics to put in storage and keep them safe."

I laughed in his face, purely out of guilt and utter desperation for sympathy, and luckily, he laughed right along with me.

That night was the end of the three commandments before they even had a chance to become set in stone, but it was the beginning of something better than the fairy tale. We had comedy – and that is more precious than perfect – fitting jeans.

*ANDREA C. is also known as the writer behind the mediocre blog, the* <u>Underachiever's Guide to Being a Domestic Goddess</u>. *Her days are filled with dishes, laundry, Legos, cats and boys; topped off with love, laughter and lots of accidental profanities. She is a fifty percent-er giving seventy percent, and not giving a hundred percent to anyone. On the inside, she is a brilliant writer and billionaire – on the outside, she is just a fun-loving mom, wife and friend trying to make her way in a world filled with too many carbs and not enough time to exercise. When she is not working in the family business, she gives her free time to several non-profit organizations dedicated to helping children and families in need. She's a contributor to several other humor anthologies including* I Just Want to Pee Alone, "You Have Lipstick on Your Teeth," *and* How Can You Laugh at a Time Like This.

# Open Letter To My Son
## (Or: Your Mother's Top Ten List of Ways Not to Be a Douchebag Husband)
### By Christine Burke
*Keeper of the Fruit Loops*

Dearest Son,

*Sigh.*

You are going to leave me someday.

*Double sigh.*

As the person who has micromanaged your entire existence for many years, it's hard for me to admit that at some point in the not so distant future, I am going to have to let you leave my loving, ~~controlling~~, supportive home and send you off into the world of marriage vows, child rearing, and Home Depot. You will have to find your way through the pitfalls of dating, the trauma of heartbreak, the pure exhilaration First Love brings and the agony when it ends, the excitement of lasting love and hopefully, if you are lucky, the joy of marriage and partnership.

Marriages and partnerships don't just happen. Rather, it takes years to hone dating skills, to learn how to dodge the girls you knew were a mistake from the beginning but you just couldn't help yourself and to eventually realize true love. Learning how to go from a "me" to an "us" can be a daunting, confusing task, especially for gentlemen. There are rules, there are nuances, there's Man Code. And Girl Code. And the "Don't Call For Three Days After a Date Rule" At least it was three days in my day. And the boy called. Because good girls didn't call boys. *Ahem.*

There will come a day, though, when finally everything you've learned about dating and love will converge and you will meet The Right Girl. The Right Girl will make you feel whole and she will make you consider not wearing the same T-shirt three days in a row. The Right Girl will help you buy a couch that doesn't smell like beer and she will put a plant in your apartment. And you'll like it. You will want to spend your life with The Right Girl and no son of mine is going screw it up. No siree, Bob.

This Future Mother In Law is not gonna let The Right Girl get away. Not on my watch, Bucko.

As with most things under the umbrella of motherhood, I take the task of molding you into prime marriage material very seriously. Not only because it's the right thing to do but also because I never want a daughter-in-law standing in my kitchen with a "Why the hell didn't you teach him not to do that to me?" look on her face. This future grandmother wants to see her grandkids and the only way that's gonna happen is if your future wife is happy. And if your future wife is happy, your mother is happy. Win-win for you, see?

So let's be clear here: as Your Mother, it's my job to make sure that you aren't an asshole to your future wife. And, because Your Mother didn't marry an asshole, let's keep the family tradition alive, shall we?

With that in mind, I've come up with a list of things that every husband or boyfriend should know ahead of time. This is a list that I've compiled over fourteen years of marriage, eight years of college and high school dating, and one awkward year of eighth grade dating, which, come to think of it, was actually more like picking partners for kickball. We are going to skip the obvious stuff that most people will tell you, like "Respect her," and "No Means No," and "You go to the door to pick her up and meet her father" because, frankly, if you try to leave my house without committing these basic tenets to memory, I will kick you until you are dead. Rather, these are less obvious, much more nuanced rules and tools that will ensure success in your relationship.

## Your Mother's Top Ten List of Ways Not to Be a Douchebag Husband

1. Acts of service will get you farther than any box of Russell Stover chocolates. Flowers are nice but emptying the dishwasher is nicer. Stopping for milk on the way home is okay but doing the entire grocery order without a call from the aisle because you can't find the pasta sauce is better. Taking one child on an errand is helpful but taking all of them ensures you can play golf tomorrow. Offering to take her out on the town is romantic, but arranging the babysitter will get you laid. Actions speak louder than flowers, my dear.

2. If it's gross, don't do it in front of her. Period. No wife on the planet wants to see you doing any of the following: wiping your ass,
bending over the toilet clipping your toenails or whacking off. Further, minimizing ball scratching, walking around in holey underwear
and nose hair clipping is advised. Some things are best left behind
closed doors. ALWAYS.

3. A gift from Victoria's Secret is never, ever a gift for her and you
know it. So don't buy her one. Ever. Sweats are sexy. Say it with me:
Sweats. Are. Sexy.

4. Understand that she will never ever love or understand your passion as much as you do. This goes for sports, *Star Wars*, anything
with the words fuel or injector in it and Minecraft. Conversely, you
will never understand her passion for *Downton Abbey*, anything related to fashion, her need to talk to her BFF about everything or her obsession with watching *90210* reruns. Just accept that you have separate interests and at least pretend to listen when she's asking you if
you think the pair of strappy sandals she's wearing matches her new
dress. And realize she's pretending to listen to you, too, while she's
chanting "Donna Martin Graduates!" (Do not roll your eyes at your
mother because she can quote every. single. episode of *Beverly Hills,
90210*. That show was cool once, you know…).

5. Always put a Dunkin Donuts gift card at the bottom of her Christmas stocking. Doing this signifies that you understand her need for
free coffee gratification. And, if the card is for twenty five bucks or
over, you get bonus points. Trust me. A Starbucks card is okay, too.

6. Sex is a two way street and it's best to learn this as early as possible. Yes, you are a man and yes, you think about sex every two point
three seconds and yes, you want it anytime, ANNNY-WHERE but
it's not just about you. She likes orgasms just as much as the next gal,
but after a day of toddler tantrums, dried baby puke, and sore

nipples, it's going to take more than just a "You wanna?". When you have kids, foreplay is less about deep sensual kissing and more about picking up the family room without being asked and offering to do the midnight feeding that night. Remember what I said about arranging a babysitter?

7. Your wife will always decide where you spend Christmas so choose wisely. And by choosing, I mean her family. And our family. Being in a relationship is a minefield of holiday bombs and it's essential that you navigate the field carefully and thoughtfully. Your family loves you. Her family loves her. You love her. She loves you. So, make sure you both love each other enough to incorporate your families into your holiday chaos. And realize that if you aren't crazy about her family, you still have to see them, Clark. Cousin Eddie exists in every family so it's best to just down the reindeer glass of eggnog and suffer through it. Cuz when you marry the girl, you marry Cousin Eddie, my dear. All bets are off if they blow up your cat, though.

8. You are responsible for the disposal of any and all spiders, bugs, creepy crawlers, mice, vermin, and snakes. It's best to accept right now that when you go away on a business trip and come home to a red Solo cup secured with a book, you will be dealing with whatever is trapped underneath. And you may not make a comment on the fact that she walked around it in the kitchen for four days. Not a word, sir. Not a word.

9. One word: forgiveness. Say it with me. Foooorrreggggivvveness. In the course of any one day in your relationship, you will be obligated to forgive no less than three offenses by your partner. No joke. And she will have to do the same for you. She will forgive you every single damned day when you don't put your dishes IN the actual dishwasher, choosing instead to put them on the counter ABOVE the dishwasher. You will have to forgive her when you are down to one last pair of clean underwear and you come home to find that she

*might* have been on the phone with her BFF dealing with a childrearing crisis for three hours. She will have to forgive you when you store car parts in the dining room, when your middle of the night fart rivals a nuclear explosion and when everything in your world stops because *Days of Thunder* is on TBS for the four hundredth time. All day long, every day, you will have to forgive the little things so that when the need to forgive the big things comes along, the forgiveness flows faster. Major Acts of Stupid require patience like no other and you cannot find that level of forgiveness if you are still harboring anger over dirty underwear and dishes.

10. This last one is a sensitive one, so hear me out. Your Mother was your first love. She's the one you promised that you'd marry when you were five. She's the one you promised you'd build a big house next door to and live there forever so she'd never be lonely. She's the one who has held your hand when you were scared of the creepy red eyes at the Statue of Liberty exhibit, the one who has saved you from bodily harm on at least thirty two separate occasions, and who cleaned up the buckets of puke you spewed in your bathroom not once but TWICE (I'm not bitter here, not bitter at all). She's the one who has loved you through your sweet, fat baby cheeks, your acne road map, and your teenaged chiseled cheekbones. She may not have always shown it the right way or in the way you understood at the time but SHE. LOVES. YOU. And she wants you to be happy. So, when you go off into the big scary world of marriage, kids, and Home Depot, remember she's always there to lend a hand. Or babysit (wink, wink, nudge, nudge). Your wife may be your eventual, lasting love, but your mom was the one you loved first. Don't forget me.

So, it's that easy.

Follow the above and you won't be a douchebag. And your wife will be happy. And, say it with me, so will Your Mother.

*Ahem.*
   With love,

   Your Mother

PS. It's your night to take out the garbage.


CHRISTINE BURKE *is the Keeper of The Fruit Loops, Manager of the Fecal Roster, and Driver of the People Mover. In other words, she's a mom. An Erma Bombeck Martha Stewart with a Roseanne twist, she has the mouth and organized cabinets to prove it. She resides in Pennsylvania with her supportive, ever budget conscious husband, her blog inspiring two Fruit Loops and her extensive collection of thrift shop shoes. In her spare time, she runs marathons, governs the PTA like nobody's business, and is still pissed NBC cancelled* **Smash.** *Her personal website is* keeperofthefruitloops.blogspot.com.

# Project Run Away
## By Raquel D'Apice
### *The Ugly Volvo*

I don't like to think of myself as a horrifically shallow person, but there are times when you're on a first date with someone and they're smiling at you, and you're smiling back at them, and you're thinking, "He seems so wonderful. He seems like such a wonderful, interesting, lovable person and why is he dressed like someone who sleeps in an ATM kiosk?"

On my first date with Jonathan, he dressed as if he had robbed a Salvation Army clothing drop and had attired himself in the first items he had found, regardless of size or appropriateness. He was tall and thin and wore oddly-shaped, faded black jeans and a T-shirt so ridiculously large that the seams that should've been by his shoulders hung near his elbows. The T-shirt said "Valparaiso, Chile" with a small picture of a sailboat and was so old that pieces of the image and some of the letters had chipped off. He covered the T-shirt with an ill-fitting Khaki jacket whose zipper appeared to be made from paperclips. I was uncertain as to whether I should kiss him or hand him a UNICEF package.

"Hi," I said. "Nice to meet you."

"Hi," he said, smiling. He had a wonderfully genuine smile which, at least for a while, distracted me from the fact that, for whatever reason, he had his pants tucked into his socks.

"Do you want to head into the restaurant?" I asked, noting that his hair appeared to have been cut by blind men using either nail clippers or butter knives.

"Sure," he said, nodding. "I'd love to."

And I am looking at him, thinking that he looks a lot like his online profile photo with the exception that in his online profile photo he was wearing a plain gray T-shirt, whereas in real life he dressed more like an eleven-year-old who has run away from home.

\*     \*     \*

"How did your date go?" a friend asked. "It went well.

He dresses worse than anyone I've ever met," I said. "But still, strangely, it went well."

It's tricky not liking how someone dresses because how they dress isn't technically their physical appearance, like the sharpness of their cheekbones or their height or their eye color. It's something impermanent, so it seems like something you can change. And you think, "Oh, well here is this lovely handsome guy who dresses worse than most eight-year-olds I've met, but it's fine because I'm sure I can change that."

And because it's a thing that can be changed, you assume it can be changed *simply*. This is a common mistake.

On our second date, he wore extremely faded blue jeans that were so large he had cinched them around his thin waist with a belt, making him look like a scarecrow that had come to life for the sole purpose of taking me to a Vietnamese restaurant. He was also wearing an extremely large T-shirt advertising the Utah Food Bank, and his hair was parted straight down the middle.

"Your hair is parted straight down the middle," I said, incredulously.

"Is it?" he asked. "Is that bad? I don't part my hair."

"You don't part your hair? It just parted itself like that?"

"I guess," he said. "I didn't do anything to it."

"You look like a blackjack dealer from the 1890's."

"Is that bad?" he asked again. He seemed suddenly nervous. Not neurotically so, but quietly anxious. I felt terrible for having brought it up.

"It's not bad," I said, smiling. "Can I fix it for you?" He nodded, and I ran my fingers through his hair which inevitably, in case you're trying this at home, will make you fall a little bit in love with a person, even if they are dressed atrociously.

Not that I (I should make this clear) had Bill Cunningham trailing any of my own wardrobe choices. For years, I myself had dressed horribly, pairing oversized pants with strange, unflattering shirts and the types of shoes normally found on a forty-nine-year-old woman with back pain. I wore strange vests or confusing attempts at period clothing. An outfit I dearly loved had once prompted someone to ask if I was auditioning for either *The Sound of Music* or a Ricola cough drop commercial.

I had no idea how to dress my body and have never followed anything related to fashion. For its first two years on the air, I thought the show *Project Runway* was about planes. The roommate of an old boyfriend of mine had eventually taken me aside:

"Look," she said. "You're a wonderful human being, but nothing you're wearing fits or, to be frank, even makes sense."

"What do you mean?" I asked, smoothing my sweater vest and straightening the long khaki skirt that sometimes caused people to mistake me for a young Hassidic woman.

"It's too difficult to explain," she said. "But we'll go out and have you try on a few things and let's see what we can do."

\*     \*     \*

When the third date arrived, he wore a black coat that must've once belonged to a man twice his height and weight because it hung off him comically, making him look like a large, black bell. He was wearing awkwardly-tapered tan pants, and there was an enormous, unpopped pimple nestled in the stubble on his chin.

"Are you ok?" he asked.

"I'm fine," I said. "You have a – " I stared at the pimple, biting my lip.

"I have a what?"

"Nothing," I said. "Sorry. It was nothing. You had a little pimple on your face."

"Oh, I have a HUGE pimple on my face," he said.

"Oh, so you saw it?"

"How could I not see it?" he asked, laughing.

"How can you see it and not get rid of it?" I asked, incredulous.

"It'll go away on its own," he said, taking my hand in his and walking toward the movie theater.

And I sat next to him through a very enjoyable showing of *Iron*

# The Ugly Volvo

*Man*, occasionally stealing frantic glances at the Mount St. Helens of facial acne because that is how I am—I am obsessive. You can be thirty feet away from me, but I promise you I am looking directly at your ingrown hairs and wishing I were pulling them out of your neck with a tweezer. Someone walking around with an enormous, unpopped pimple on his face is like a dentist office with a giant, askew picture frame in the waiting room. I can only sit there for so long before looking at it drives me to either remedy the situation or lose my mind thinking about it.

*Iron Man* ended and we stood outside the theater, facing one another.

"That was great," I said.

"It was," he said. "Do you want to make plans to do dinner again soon?"

I looked at him—a giant, black Liberty bell with tiny, tan ankles and a pimple so prominent it may as well have been surrounded by arrows and flashing lights. I wanted to bury my face in my hands. He was dressed so badly. He was dressed so, so badly it made me cringe, and he had such a kind face and such a caring, beautiful, genuine smile that looking at it made me like living in the world more.

"Yes," I said. "I'd love to see you again."

He smiled.

"Are you free tomorrow?" he asked as he looked at me lovingly.

I looked back at his chin, distracted by his enormous pimple, anxiously grinding my teeth.

\*　　\*　　\*

Jonathan and I met the next day in Washington Square Park, and he was wearing vomit-colored hiking pants that zipped off into shorts, a T-shirt so small that the collar threatened to cut off his air supply, and a red plaid button-down shirt that—I fell silent for a moment.

"You look great," I said, dumbfounded. "Where did you get that shirt?"

"What shirt?" Jonathan asked. He seemed to barely notice that he was wearing clothes at all. He looked down at himself. "This one?" he asked, motioning to the red button-down.

"Yes."

"An ex-girlfriend bought it for me. She said I didn't have anything that fit."

"You don't," I said, sighing.

"Well, that's why you're so wonderful," he said, smiling, holding my hand. "Because you don't mind."

And here is the part that felt like someone taking screwdrivers and thrusting them into my abdomen, twisting them until my blood and organs came rushing out. Because here is the part where you either lie and say you don't mind when in actuality you are bothered by it every fifteen minutes, or you knowingly hurt someone very sweet and kind—someone who seems to care for you more than anyone in your history of dating has ever seemed to care for you. Someone who, you're starting to realize, is the type of person you were, maybe, hoping to spend your life with.

"I do mind a little," I said quietly.

His face fell. He stopped smiling and immediately looked worried.

"Look," I said. "This is important. You are a wonderful person. You are smart and funny. You're handsome. But sometimes when you're wearing clothing that's ten sizes too big for you, it's harder to see those other things." I paused. "Do you remember what you said about my online profile?" I asked.

"What about it?"

"The thing you said you hated about it," I said.

"Oh, the quotes," he said. "All the Daniel Day Lewis *There Will Be Blood* quotes were weird."

"Ok," I said. "Clearly I made a mistake including quotes from *There Will be Blood* on an online dating profile. I thought it was funny at the time. I didn't really think that through all the way."

"It was just sort of strange and weird. A little uncomfortable," he said quietly, politely.

"I know," I said, hanging my head. "I'm strange and uncomfortable a lot. And I was so happy you decided to write to me and meet up anyway. But imagine," I continued, "if every time we met up, I kept reciting lines from that movie. If every time you leaned in to kiss me I went, *'I'm an oil man, ladies and gentlemen. This is my son and partner H.W.'* and if every time you smiled at me from across a restaurant table I went, *'I drink your milk shake!'* and if every time you reached out to hold my hand I went, *'You are not the chosen brother, Eli!'*"

"I wouldn't love it," he admitted.

"Ok," I said. "So that's how you're dressed. I don't love it. But it doesn't stop me from realizing how sweet and kind and wonderful you are. From thinking you're funny. From realizing you're such a good person. From wanting to go on another date with you even though this date technically hasn't started yet."

Jonathan allowed himself a small smile.

"Would you like to meet up for dinner later this week," I asked him, grinning.

"Assuming this date goes well?" he said.

"Assuming this date goes well."

"What days work well for you?" he asked.

"How about tomorrow?" I said, and he grinned.

*     *     *

It is a few months later and we're at Jonathan's apartment, going through his closet.

"Can we get rid of these?" I ask him, holding up a pair of pale, plaid boxer shorts that appear to have been ravaged by a baby wolverine.

"I guess those have seen better days," he says.

"What about this T-shirt?" I ask.

"It's a little small?" he says, guessing, pulling the shirt over his head.

"By 'a little small' do you mean 'when you wear it people can see your bellybutton and you look like the lovechild of Barbara Eden and a werewolf?"

"So no," he said.

"No," I replied.

And the next thing I pull from his closet makes him frown a little —it is an enormous cable-knit sweater. The label marks it as XXXL. For the record, Jonathan is 6'2" and 145 pounds, which – if you're not good with visualizing people – means he has the body type of a churro. He can draw a stick figure and it will double as a self-portrait.

"I wear that sweater a lot," he said. "It's really big and comfy—I normally wear it when I'm writing or doing stuff around the house." He placed it lovingly over his head. " Also, it's really warm. I want to make sure I don't get rid of all my warm sweaters."

"Look," I said slowly. "I appreciate how much of your stuff you've been willing to get rid of. So I don't want to seem ungrateful. And if you really want to hold onto this sweater, you can. But…" I said.

"But?"

And with that, I walked toward him and slowly, carefully, climbed into the sweater alongside him so that both our arms snaked through the sleeves, our hands palm to palm protruding from the cuffs. Slowly, carefully, I pushed my head through the neck hole, inches from his face. We stood for several seconds, both of us wearing the sweater, our heads face to face, jutting from the collar like confused Siamese twins.

"I'm not saying you shouldn't be comfortable," I said, "but I just want to highlight the fact that both of us are inside this sweater right now. And it's not even tight."

"Maybe it is a little big," he conceded, his mouth inches from my face.

"It's the size of a one-bedroom apartment," I said.

"It is sort of like a one-bedroom apartment," he agreed. "Is that a hint that you'd like to move in with me?"

He was smiling. He was almost always smiling. And I looked at his head, two inches away from my own, with his crazy hair that parted itself down the middle like Flat Top from *Dick Tracy*, protruding from a sweater so large it could double as a nuclear-missile silo. Moving in with him would mean living with someone who didn't tweeze the hairs between his eyebrows and who owned sweaters that could provide shelter for a nomadic family of four. It would mean waking up every morning next to someone who slept in clothes so large they could be mistaken for the sheets and whose "dress clothes" consisted of a wool blazer so wide in the shoulders he looked like a four-year-old dressed up as a used-car salesman. Studying his face, I saw the beginnings of another pimple beginning on his cheek.

"If I moved in with you, could I pop that pimple?" I asked, reaching slowly for his face, forcing his own arms, which were still in the sleeves, to reach for it as well.

"Absolutely not," he said. He was smiling.

"All right then," I said. "I'd love to." And with that, he pulled his arms from the sleeves and wrapped them around me, kissing me gently on the face, our heads still protruding from the sweater. Elated, I closed my eyes and leaned in to the kiss.

I loved him so much. And with my eyes closed, it didn't even matter that he had tucked his pants into his socks again.

*RAQUEL D'APICE is a stand-up comedian and writer who keeps a blog called The Ugly Volvo, best known for the post, "A 10 Month Old's Letter to Santa." Her writing and humor have been featured in Slate,* The Huffington Post, *BUST Magazine and Reader's Digest. She lives in Jersey City, New Jersey with her husband, young son, and lingering feelings of inadequacy.*

# The Problem With the Hands-On Father
## By Amy Flory
### *Funny Is Family*

"Please let this work," I pray, as I sandwich my head between two pillows. My exhausted body hums with anxiety and desperation while my nerves burn.

I roll over, and wedge my ears deeper into the cocoon of cotton and polyester, but the sound still follows. It wiggles into my brain, this cross between a screeching owl and the dull moan of an oncoming train, and it makes the hair on my arms stand on end.

Nature's way of ensuring a mother tends to her child is incredibly powerful, but right now it's driving me mad. My husband is in the other room, attempting to soothe our newborn son, hell bent on bonding with his boy, and every time my son wails, I am fighting my maternal instinct to go to him. To soothe him. To comfort him.

I am tired. I want a nap, but that will never happen if I can hear my son crying for me.

"I don't like passing off a crying baby," my husband said. "If I always give him to you when he cries, what happens when you aren't here?"

"But he wants me," I whined. "I'm his *mother*."

"And I'm his father. We'll be fine. Go take a nap."

This hands-on approach from my loving husband turned doting father is what led me to my pillow-head sandwich, which, with the addition of two more pillows, has become a double-decker.

In theory, this is wonderful. I knew my husband would be a hands-on father, and so far, three weeks into his role, he's killing it. He changed the first diaper in the hospital, and many since. He isn't afraid of holding our boy, even though that child flops around like a wet noodle with a bobblehead, and still weighs in at a measly six pounds.

But what the hell is happening out there? I know our baby isn't hungry. He just drained my milk bags dry. He should be settling in for a nap, but instead he sounds like a bag of cats - angry, feral cats, sent to drive me over the edge.

Maybe this is my punishment for being so smug. I remember thinking, "Oh, your husband wasn't much interested in your kids until they were a little older, when they could smile and hold a ball, and say Dada?" I pitied those women. My man has tons of experience with babies, and even helped raise his youngest siblings.

Not that I really liked newborns before I had one. They look like half-bird, half-humans. Plus, they seem so fragile. I can be counted on to break at least one thing per day, and generally like to save my daily allowance of destruction for things that are particularly irreplaceable and special. Almost everyone considers their baby to be both. For this reason alone, I can't be trusted to hold newborns.

My husband, on the other hand, comes from a family that is crazy about babies in the same way I'm crazy about meatball subs. They would eat them whole if they could. They cradle them lovingly and aren't afraid of dropping them. Even when there are enough babies for everyone to hold one, they still find a way to complain that someone is being a baby hog.

My baby daddy loves kids so much, that just a week after our son was born he suggested we start trying for another. "This is fun," he grinned, as he held our sleeping son and I held cabbage leaves on my throbbing breasts. "Let's do it again. We just have to wait six weeks, right?" His earnest suggestion made me want to have my legs surgically sewed together for at least a year, but maybe today's cryfest will help him see things clearly. Maybe I won't have to talk my doctor into making me look like a mermaid until I'm ready for another round of being an upside down human PEZ dispenser.

As I squeeze my legs tightly together, I hear it. Silence.

I peek my head out of my pillow bunker, adjust the greasy ponytail that has landed me the nickname "slick pony" and listen. The wails wind up again, and I peek at the clock before diving back undercover. Three minutes have passed.

I bury my head as deep as it will go, and I scream, loud and long. It takes the edge off.

I'll bet that son of a bitch is sitting down. He knows the baby settles more easily when we stand, but he stubbornly refuses to get up.

## I Just Want to Be Alone

Please, Lord, give my boy his father's intelligence and tenacity, but not his willfulness.

This prayer is too late, isn't it?

Maybe I should leave the house? Where would I go? Would I have to wear pants? I'll give it two more minutes, and then I'm ripping that baby out of his hands like a Super Bowl football with the game on the line. My son may not be hungry, but he wants his momma. I've had about enough of this shit, and my husband, the skilled scientist, has had his chance. From now on, he can keep his experiments in the lab, and not with our kids.

But isn't parenthood one big experiment? Don't we just follow our instincts, utilize expert opinions when making decisions, and cross our fingers that we don't fuck them up too much?

I wrack my brain. What do the experts say about dads and babies? That moms need to allow them to form their own relationships and not micromanage? That sounds reasonable, but what about the crying? I wonder what the world's record for a baby's crying jag is, and are we almost there?

Four minutes.

How can he even stand it? Maybe he left like I want to? Is that why my sweet boy is crying? Just last week we ran to Blockbuster to grab a movie and almost left the driveway before we remembered we had a baby sleeping in the other room, and we couldn't leave him home alone. Babies are different from dogs in that way, apparently.

The dog! Maybe our even-tempered black lab has snapped in the same way I am about to, and he attacked the baby. Maybe my dog and my husband battled to the death, leaving my child out there alone, in the middle of the carnage.

Those women who are married to the type of man who doesn't engage with his kids are so lucky. I'd give my right nut for a douchey asshole who spends more time golfing than at home, and when he is home, he isn't helping or engaging his family. I used to be pissed at Adam Corolla, of television and radio fame, for proudly refusing to ever change a diaper, but now he looks positively dreamy.

I mean, the diaper changing is nice, but I would change every diaper in the entire world if the incessant howling of the fruit of my womb would cease. That's a fair trade.

I peek my head out again. Quiet.

Shit, do I actually have to do all that diaper changing now? That was hyperbole, not a real trade. I didn't sign anything, and I didn't shake on it. I'll have to call my husband's younger sisters. Those bitches love changing my son's diapers. Like I said, that family is crazy about babies.

The clock says it's been six minutes. I lie there, unmoving, and listen.

Silence.

I ease out of bed, pushing the hair off my face so I look less like a character from *Fraggle Rock* and more like a human being, and softly open our bedroom door.

My husband is in his recliner, with our sleeping boy on his chest. "Five minutes," he brags, looking at me triumphantly. "Told you I could do it."

"Six," I reply, flopping on the sofa. "We need thicker pillows."


*AMY FLORY and her husband made two kids, a four-year-old girl and a six-year-old boy. She does not consider herself a housewife, as she owns no pearls and only one apron. Amy is a* Huffington Post *blogger, has been featured on various parenting and humor websites, writes for her local newspaper, and is a contributing author to* "You Have Lipstick on Your Teeth", *and* I Just Want to Pee Alone. *She was named one of Mashable's 17 Funny Moms on Twitter, but her kids still think Dad is "the funny one." Amy writes embarrassing stories about her family and herself at* Funny Is Family.

# I've Been Duped
# By Stephanie Young
## *I'm Still Learning*

My husband reeled me in with his chivalry, won me over with his charm, and made me believe I was marrying the most romantic guy on earth. Then once the rings were on, he quickly reached his Romantic Quota, and just *stopped*. He pulled the old bait and switch, and I fell for it—hook, line, and sinker!

Back in college when we first met, he had a colossal crush on me—pretty much from day one. It was no secret, either: he'd walk me to class, carry my books, buy me stuffed animals, and so on.

His charm was lost on me at first; I simply had no romantic interest in him, whatsoever. You see, my husband was a nice guy—a nineteen-year-old, wise-beyond-his-years (yet slightly awkward), nice guy. He believed the way to a girl's heart was through selfless gestures, kindness, and courtesy.

But sadly, I was not attracted to those character traits. No, this flighty, immature eighteen-year old girl preferred the jerky guy. The guy who ignored her. The guy who rarely fussed over her. The guy who made her work for his unworthy attention.

A pathetic state of affairs, I know. But I was young and unwise to the ways of adulthood and common sense.

Though I was well aware of (and, I hate to admit, kind of relished in) his infatuation with me, I never led him on. I was very clear from the outset that I did not return the feelings, but very much enjoyed having him as a close friend—and he was (seemingly) okay with that.

But that didn't stop him; he was relentless. *Romantically relentless.* On my nineteenth birthday, he surprised me with the most unbelievable gift. You see, it was my first birthday away from home and I had been feeling a little homesick. Determined to make my birthday a memorable one, he gathered up a bunch of our mutual friends for a little birthday dinner at a local restaurant. And just as we were about to leave, he had the waiters bring out an adorable, one foot tall, black and white panda bear birthday cake—a cake that he'd asked his mom, a semi-professional baker, to whip up for me.

## I'm Still Learning

*Wow.*

He clearly deserved better; I didn't give him the time of day, yet he was perfection—going to all this trouble to impress a girl who only wanted to be his friend.

*What was I thinking?*

But in the end, his efforts paid off—and he eventually mesmerized me into a romantic stupor. I fell madly in love. And after he and his panda cake exploits won me over, he turned up the volume on his charm even more.

He wrote poems that made me swoon, bought me beautiful "just because" jewelry, and regularly took me on surprise romantic outings. He was free-flowing with the *I-love-you*s and always held my hand in public. He dedicated songs to me on the radio, happily accompanied me to chick flicks, and made it a regular practice to open the car door for me. When we talked on the phone, he actually talked —and listened. Like, for hours!

A guy! Talking! It was the stuff dreams are made of.

He was pure gold; I'd scored me a genuine Prince Charming.

Six years later, we were married—and even during the early years of our marriage, his thoughtful gestures were still sweeping me off my feet. On our first wedding anniversary, he surprised me with exactly what I had hoped for: a top-of-the-line garbage disposal for our new home.

A garbage disposal!

Okay, ladies. Seriously. What girl *wouldn't* love that? What new homeowner girl wouldn't love a machine that allowed her to simply throw bits of rotten food down the sink only to have it disappear forever? (To this day, that precious garbage disposal is probably the best gift I've ever received.)

I was married to the perfect man.

But alas, the perfection came to an end. My husband's romantic tendencies slowly went into hiding like a scared little child afraid of the boogieman. He replaced his tender loving, over-the-top thoughtful side with a much less enjoyable we've-been-together-forever-now-so-I-no-longer-have-to-woo-you-with-romantic-crap side.

Enter: another birthday memory. My thirty-fifth. We'd been married eight years at this point. A far cry from the one sixteen years earlier, this birthday gave birth to a whole new type of gift from my husband: the verbal gift. Yes, this lucky girl was the proud recipient of the "how about you go out and buy yourself that camera you've been talking about" gift. No *actual* gift. No card. No breakfast in bed. No flowers. No dinner out. No day off from doing dishes. No reprieve from yelling kids. No special treatment, whatsoever.

Didn't he understand that my relentlessly talking about said camera was a blatant hint that I'd wanted him to actually go out and buy it, wrap it and, you know... hand it to me? Make the eentsy weensy bit of effort it would take to make me happy? A little friggin' forethought, perhaps?

And since when did it become acceptable to not bother getting your wife a card on her birthday?

*I get to go buy myself my own birthday gift? Gee, thanks! Should I get my own card, bake my own cake and sing myself "Happy Birthday" while I'm at it?*

I was duped. Bamboozled. Hoodwinked. He reeled me at the start with his unrelenting adoration and now this?

His true identity was finally revealed, and with it I was left to my own devices—scouring internet for my own birthday treats.

Today, my husband is about a romantic as a tree stump.

Sure, growing older, having kids, and settling into the monotony of marriage can suck the romantic passion out of people. I get it. But this is a bit extreme, no? It's almost like he knew at a very young age what he wanted (me), went after it with an unrelenting drive and, in doing so, depleted his stores of romantic ingenuity. He didn't pace himself and now I'm paying the price.

But that's okay; I've sort of gotten used to it—and I've adjusted accordingly: I leave him sticky notes with gift ideas or reminders to pay me compliments, I tell our boys to remind him when a birthday or anniversary is approaching, and sometimes when I'm feeling the need for a little pick-me-up, I'll shoot him a text asking him to grab me a "surprise" bouquet of flowers (which almost always come from the grocery store on his way home from work).

Marriage: ain't it grand?

My husband and I have been together twenty one years, married fourteen. And though happily married, I often long to go back to a time when he had it in him to lie awake at night conjuring up grand romantic schemes involving panda bear confections and shiny garbage disposals.

Hmm. I wonder if time travel machines really do exist. Maybe I'll check on Amazon the next time I'm buying myself a gift to sign his name to.


*STEPHANIE YOUNG is the mom of two animated boys, wife to one cigar-loving sports fanatic and writer behind the blog, I'm Still Learning. Her goal in life is to find the calm amidst the crazy—which, given the dominance of testosterone in her house, is usually hidden in some obscure corner of her home. In addition to musing about the adventures of parenthood and the rollercoaster that is marriage, Stephanie enjoys writing on the topics of physical health and emotional wellness. Stephanie is also the author of the book, How to Eat Healthy Without Noticing: A Non-Dieter's Guide to Eating Better.*

# Bring on the Bees
## By Meredith Spidel
### *The Mom of the Year*

I love my husband. I love who he is and what he stands for. I admire what he does and how he spends his time on this earth. Except for the bees.

You see, my husband is a good man.

He's my best friend.

Spending time with him? Love it.

While all this blissful marital togetherness is super, there's one sticky wicket: I like my alone time. *A lot.* Privacy for me? *A very good thing.* And with two young ones in the mix, mmm ... let's just say solitude is a rare event. Having more time to pee alone most assuredly remains the greatest goal of my thirties. It can happen, right? Dreams do come true? *Just say yes.*

Because of this, I have always been a fan of my husband's hobbies. The fact that he has them, pursues them, and rarely requires no more of me than cheerleading from the sidelines works out extremely well for us. If there's any spare time after the kids are in bed and he is tinkering around, pass me my newest loan from the library, and I am a happy woman. He can do his thing, and I can focus on my reading and things like remembering to brush my teeth. Win-win for everybody.

While his hobby habit is a delight, it can get *intense* at times. The range of his obsessions appears to know no bounds. In the fifteen years that we've been together, he has taken up backpacking, woodworking, hunting, fishing, volleyball, chess, plumbing, oenology, camping, foosball, gardening, genealogy, hiking, tennis, billiards, and homebrewing. He is a terrific bass guitar player and he makes his own vanilla extract. He's into DIY home-repair and is in the process of finishing our basement.

Fine. No sweat. I can go with the flow and wrap my head around whatever is the latest and greatest ... usually. To his credit, he generally adopts each new hobby with commitment. Often a *vigorous* commitment and figures out a way to do it on the super-cheap.

*Smart man.*

Most of these endeavors benefit our entire family in some way and are just plain cool. Having a stash of award-winning home brews to share with friends? Awesome. And the garden crops have saved us a boatload of money. Not to mention the veggies are *tasty*.

The hobbies then tend to get abandoned when they no longer fit – i.e. when our son was born as the most colicky infant ever, the lengthy backpacking trips made Mommy a "little grouchy." Wood-crafting has gotten the boot until a proper space for The Tools (any woman worth her salt knows this must be capitalized) can be set up in our transitioning basement.

Flux and flow of life … sure, I can be on board. Until …

*Until …*

BEE-KEEPING.

*Yes, you read that right.* When my husband first came home and announced he wanted to start sheltering up the little buzzers, I pulled the old acknowledge-ignore trick. Where you just mumble recognition of the words coming out of his mouth, while actually thinking he's insane, and then literally hold your breath in silence until he hopefully forgets about it? Yeah that. I did that.

He worked himself up into an in-love-with-the-idea frenzy. He got his bestie on board, billing it as a fun outdoor activity they could enjoy together while creating a healthy natural product. How was I supposed to argue with this? The dedication deepened; they signed up for meetings through the State Bee Keepers Association. Worse? He wanted to actually *go* to these meetings. This was not looking good.

I grew increasingly fearful by the minute. I considered somehow hacking the Internet and permanently shutting down any bee-keeping related sites. Upon realizing my knowledge of computer programming extends to restarting my computer when something starts blinking, I had to forgo this idea and just pour a glass of wine instead. And pray the whole bee scenario would somehow magically fade off his radar.

But the man wouldn't be deterred from his mission. And he was fighting with savvy on this one. He started in on the gentle, indicating that the bees would be kept on his friend's property, several miles from our home. I still wasn't in love with the idea, but at least I would have no immediate contact with the bees, right?

Or not ...

He somehow pulled a sneaky shift. He began discussing housing the hives in our yard. Worse, when I called him out on this location change, he acted like I had lost my marbles and he had always been planning to keep them at our home. *Well-played, husband, well-played.* Bizarre and unusual hardware began filling our Amazon cart. What the heck is a Steel Frame Lifter and Scraper? Crap if I know. Maybe it's time for a second glass of that wine?

In any case, in a wicked smart battle move, he had clearly established his ground. Worse? He had invested in it, mentally, that is. Any objections from this point would now be an assault on his dream. *Darn him.*

I said I *love* my husband.

I didn't say I always *like* him.

Also? Sometimes I just wish he was dumb.

He is not. *Unfortunately.*

Returning to the war front, I found myself faced with the reality of bees and a whole lot of new shiny tools that made no sense to me. I pleaded the "children will surely die of a violent stinging attack" card. He noted that honeybees are not aggressive. So then I tried the "but surely the neighbors will be upset" route. He is convinced they will neither notice nor care. His parents must have turned off the VCR before the end of *My Girl.*

My ground for argument was slipping. The only thing that made me joyous at this point was thinking about how ridiculous he will look in that hyped-up all-inclusive white bee-keeper suit. *That* is good news. And there will be *a lot* of pictures. Promise.

Yet, there we were. There were bees. He was craving them. What was a gal to do? An extensive pro-con list could have been written. Except, instead of doing something productive like this, it was more fun to spend the last few moments before crashing at night trolling for cheap Urban Decay cosmetics online. *What if Macy's had a sudden flash seventy percent off sale?*

I'm his partner in this life, and this was something that has become important to him. Even if I would prefer to have shipped him off to the loony bin rather than keep these vicious creatures by the swing set, the ring twirling stubbornly around my finger indicated that maybe I had a responsibility to do otherwise. Maybe, just *maybe,* I needed to pick back up those pom-poms and cheer this dude on.

Plus, honey *is* sort of delicious.

You see, I've done my share of "off" things. I've started a blog out of thin air and then virtually pledged every free waking moment to its continuance. I have loved on my online yard-saling more than is normal for a sane person. I have taken up knitting. At age thirty-four. *Knitting.* I know.

So yes, maybe the bees were meant to be. For the time being, they may need to be a part of my world. While I might not love nor understand the blasted creatures, had I not signed up for this with the whole "I do" situation?

And let's not forget the bonus – more of that precious alone time for me. So I did it, I bought him a bee-keeping book for Christmas. And if I somehow talk him out of this folly before it comes to full realization? Even if he just holes up and reads the darn book for one night, at least I'll get an evening of some sweet uninterrupted teethbrushing for me. Maybe I'll even work in a private pee. Yes, dreams really *do* come true.

*MEREDITH SPIDEL blogs at <u>The Mom of the Year</u>, earning her title one epic parenting fail at a time. She is an author in the best-selling anthologies I Just Want to Pee Alone and "You Have Lipstick on Your Teeth." When her kids aren't busy pummeling each other with Legos or requiring their 16th sippy cup refill of the day, she tries to offer quick, relatable laughs for fellow parents and all their empathizers. She remains entirely terrified by crafts, promises to never share any useful household tips, and is fully committed to a less serious look at the world of parenting. Social media is beyond her comprehension, but she makes a pass at <u>Twitter</u> and <u>Facebook</u>.*

# The Incompetent Husband
## By Deva Dalporto
### *MyLifeSuckers*

The other day I asked my husband to pick up some potato chips from the store. He came home with a bag of tortilla chips. I repeat, tortilla chips. As in, not potato chips. I was devastated. I had been fantasizing about the potato chips ever since he left the house twenty minutes before. I had my whole evening planned out. Me, *Orange is the New Black*, and a bag of potato chips. And now it was all shot to hell.

"I wanted potato chips, not tortilla chips, honey," I said, trying to sound reasonable and keep the rising panic out of my voice. "What's the difference?" he responded. And with that—that simple, short phrase—I lost it.

"WHAT'S THE DIFFERENCE? What do you mean, 'What's the difference?' They're two entirely different things."

"No, they're not. They're both chips."

"Two different genera of chips. Two difference species. One is made out of potatoes, the other is made out of corn. One is salty and crunchy and exactly what I was craving in my exhausted I-spend-too-much-time-with-a-toddler state, the other is not. One is great just as is, the other needs to be smothered in salsa to be edible. And WE DON'T HAVE ANY SALSA!!"

Despite my pointing out the obvious difference between a potato chip and a tortilla chip, my husband refused to budge. "They're the same thing," he insisted over and over. Now thems fighting words. They're not the same thing. No human being on this planet thinks potato chips and tortilla chips are interchangeable. Including my husband.

Here's the deal. I know he bought the wrong chips on purpose. It's all a big ploy. He did it so I wouldn't ask him to go to the store anymore.

I swear my husband pretends to be incompetent at things so that he can get out of doing them. Like laundry. He's perfectly capable of tossing some like-colored items into the machine, dumping in a scoop of detergent and pressing "on." But no. The one time I asked him to toss in a load in the past ten years and, oops, he throws in a brand-new, never-before-washed red shirt into a load of whites. My son cried for weeks that all his socks were pink. And dishes. He chips and slams and bangs every dish he washes. My coffee cups are speckled with pockmarks and coated with a thin film of grease every time he "washes" them. And grocery shopping. He's the worst at grocery shopping.

Every time he goes to the store it's a four hour ordeal during which he calls me dozens of times with questions like: "What kind of pasta did you say?" and "How many apples?" and, my favorite, "Where is the checkout stand?"

When he finally drags his ass back to the house, he always looks like he's been through the Battle of Waterloo. He's sweaty, his hair is mussed and he's got a faraway, dazed look in his eyes. And of course, he's inevitably bought all the wrong things.

Now, just to be clear, my husband is no dummy. He has a Masters degree in Nuclear Engineering from M.I.T. So I don't buy his, "I'm too incompetent to go to the store" crap for a second. You're telling me you know how to change out the plutonium rods on a nuclear power plant but you can't pick up some chicken cutlets for dinner? I call B.S.

I think it's a massive conspiracy many husbands around the globe are participating in to get out of doing the crap of domestic life. Something they learn in their "man training" before they waltz down the aisle, beaming at the woman they know is going to buy toilet paper for them for the next sixty years. Why do you think they all look so happy on their wedding days?

The truth is, I'd much rather run to the store myself, get what I need, and zip home. It's better than spending forty minutes coaching him on the phone through his walk down the supermarket aisles only to have him return with all the wrong stuff. BUT, I'm not letting him off the hook that easily. I don't care if it takes him six hours and gives him a heart attack every time he has to go to the store, he's going. I don't like the doldrums of domestic life any more than he does.

I Just Want to Be Alone

But I do it all—the laundry, the dishes, the shopping—without saying peep.

And this should serve as your warning, honey. We're hip to you. We all know you know the difference between a potato chip and a tortilla chip. The gig is up.

Now. Where are my Pringles?

*DEVA DALPORTO is an actor, parenting writer, blogger and extremely tired mom of two adorable life suckers. You can read all about them on her blog, MyLifeSuckers.com. Deva is the creator of the viral video parodies "Let It Go – Mom Parody" and "What Does the Kid Say." She is a former Senior Editor for Nickelodeon's ParentsConnect where she wrote thousands of articles on things like snot and ear infections. Deva's writing has also been featured on Yahoo! Shine, Scary Mommy, What The Flicka and WeAreTeachers.com and she has produced videos for NickMom, Nickelodeon's ParentsConnect, WeAreTeachers and Zecco.com. You can join her madness on Facebook, Twitter, Pinterest, YouTube and Google+.*

# Keeping It Hot and Heavy
## By Katie Manley
### *Somewhat Sane Mom*

I was talking to this kid a few weeks ago. Well, she is in her mid-twenties and I am in my mid-thirties, so can I call her kid? Is it sad that I think of her as a kid?

Anywho, this girl is recently engaged. It should be an exciting, wonderful time in a relationship. Sure, maybe planning a wedding is stressful at times and you are wondering if it's all worth it. And it's great to vent about it to friends. But she was complaining about her fiancé, like the kind of complaining only a "married for several years" kind of gal has any business doing. I'm talking the already getting annoyed with the way he breathes kind of complaining. I wanted to say, "Hold up Sweetie, you have serious problems if you are at *this level* of complaining so early in the relationship. At this point, it should still be hot and heavy … like, at least ninety percent of the time."

Back when my husband and I were dating, then engaged, there might have been some disagreements. But I can barely remember them. It was more like, "Ugh, I don't feel like Mexican again tonight, pick a different restaurant!" or "You didn't compliment me on my new outfit from Express (that looks almost exactly like my old outfit from Express). You don't even notice me anymore!" or "What do you mean you don't care about the centerpieces for the tables at our wedding reception? How can you be so indifferent to this major life decision?"

I remember we would literally email each other (because texting wasn't that big twelve years ago) all day long. We got a new puppy and called her "our little girl." Then we would see each other all weekend and by 7:43 on Monday morning we would be emailing about how much we missed each other. We spent as much time together as possible and, get this, we watched television together almost EVERY NIGHT.

We even had a date night every Tuesday. Seriously…what young, childless couple needs a freaking date night midweek, every single week? We need one now … and that happens, like NEVER. I always find it amusing when I read articles saying you should "date" your husband to keep it fresh. Uh yeah, that's great and all...but who the hell wants to watch my three kids once a week so my husband and I can go have overpriced margaritas at Chili's? I don't know about others with young children, but people aren't exactly breaking down our door to babysit. Plus that shit gets expensive if you have to pay a babysitter. I'll tell you what, that babysitting racket makes a mint. I'm about to quit my teaching job and babysit two nights a week.

And I shit you not, back in the day I used to love when my husband (then boyfriend) left his t-shirt at my house because I would smell it when we weren't together. I would pick up his smelly ass t-shirt that he wore to play hockey and sniff it.

Now I still smell his shirts. How else would I know if I need to wash them or not?

You see ... slowly, things evolve.

Emails go from "Hey baby, can't wait to see you tonight" to text messages like "Hey babe, can you pick up baby wipes and Miralax on the way home? The baby is constipated again." or "Did you put the trash out by the curb this morning?" Dinners out go from leisurely sipping on wine and savoring an appetizer for thirty minutes to sitting down and ordering the whole meal with your drinks. Oh, and you can bring out the chicken fingers ASAP? And do you have a few packs of crackers to keep this one quiet until the chicken fingers come? She must be eating something at every damn second during our meal to remain content.

Winter nights used to mean cuddling on the sofa and watching a movie together. Suddenly ten years have passed and you find yourself on the couch alone, eating a box of white cheddar Cheez-its, crying while watching an episode of *Undercover Boss* while your other half is in the basement with his brother yelling about a hockey game. You go down to tell him how touching the episode was because this particular boss gave Antonio fifteen grand for a dream vacation and a management position only to realize that his eyes are glazing over from lack of interest in your story. Then it becomes crystal clear that he doesn't give a damn.

But that's okay.

We still keep it hot and heavy. Yes, maybe those are hot flashes. And maybe I am still carrying around the extra thirty pounds of "baby weight" from three years ago. But we are hot and heavy nonetheless.

I have accepted that we have different interests. We like our time alone. We don't have to email or text each other ALL DAY long. I don't mind if he wants to watch football for the majority of the day on Sunday. That just means that I can watch back to back episodes of *House Hunters* and bitch about how picky these assholes are that are looking for the perfect house that MUST have two sinks in the en-suite or it's a deal breaker. I mean, for real, where do they find these people? We have one sink in our ONE bathroom that is usually covered in toothpaste ... and yet we somehow survive.

These days hot and heavy can mean him emptying the dishwasher or bringing home a bottle of wine after a long day. It can mean sleeping together, actually *sleeping*, without a toddler in the middle of the bed and a small foot in your clavicle for the majority of the night. It can mean a dinner out without the kids at a restaurant that does not serve grilled cheese. Or it can mean making the most of those three minutes and twenty four seconds alone before the kids realize you are missing. You know ... *bow chicka bow* ... "MOMMY, *where are you?*"

Sure, there are disagreements in *all* relationships, young and old. Sometimes they are fight to the death, not going down without a good struggle, kind of fights over things like WHO PUT THE MILK BACK IN THE FRIDGE WITH ONLY A FEW DROPS LEFT? Or fights over who forgot to pay the cable bill because FOR THE LOVE OF ALL THAT IS HOLY, the three-year-old can't miss an episode of *Bubble Guppies*. And when there are big fights, they better be worth it because who has the energy to fight over stupid shit anyway?

I remember the other day when my husband went to do a load of laundry and SURPRISE, I forgot to change the load over from the washer to the dryer. I mean, this shit happens all the time. It's just that usually I am the one to discover my mistake. And after rewashing the same load three days in a row, I finally get my act together and rectify the situation. Well, this time my husband freaked out and was all, "How hard can it be to put the clothes in the dryer?" Instead of fueling the argument, I quietly ran the washer one more time, switched the load over to the dryer, and was on my way. I like to pride myself in knowing when an issue is not worth fighting over. When it's not worth it, I choose to bite my tongue ... or to make passive aggressive comments under my breath all day long. Either way, it seems to be a successful strategy.

So as I listened to that young, cute, stretch mark free twenty-something complain about her fiancé, I let my mind wander back in time. I didn't give any of those annoying "Just wait until you are three kids deep" warnings. I just listened. I tried not to judge. I thought about what I needed from Target and what color of L'Oreal preference I should pick to cover up my ever-multiplying gray roots. And then I made a promise to myself right then and there to try to go back to those days a bit ... "bring the sexy back," if you will.

Just because we have been together for almost a dozen years and will be married for 10 this summer doesn't mean we can't keep it young and fresh. It's time to make a point to go on those recommended "dates" ... or to find time alone, even if it means installing locks on the outside of my children's bedroom doors. Okay, I'm just kidding. I'm not really going to lock them in their rooms. But ... if they are contently playing in there and I just lock it for ten short little minutes without them knowing, is that really all that bad? It's something to consider.

So starting tonight, I think I will make out with my husband. I swear. I will allot the five minutes between the kids finally keeping their asses in bed and the beginning of *Downton Abbey* for making out. I might even shave my legs. If that isn't keeping hot and heavy, I don't know what is.

## Somewhat Sane Mom

*KATIE MANLEY is a mom to three fabulous girls, a wife, and a special education teacher who was born and raised in Delaware. In her spare time (or when she wants to ignore her kids), she likes to write for her blog Somewhat Sane Mom, watch reality television, and taste test various brands of white wine. She is the proud owner of a sweet minivan and believes that everyone should come on over to the dark side and purchase one. She loves having three daughters, but don't you dare tell her to start saving for their weddings. Education comes first. Plus, she spends all of her extra money at Target anyway.*

# I Just Want Him to Pee Alone (and Not in Bed With Me)
## By Michelle Newman
### *You're My Favorite Today*

Last year my husband wet the bed.

Or for about twelve hours he *thought* he wet the bed, which was pretty much just as bad — and disturbing — for both of us.

Since my kids were never chronic bed-wetters and have long surpassed the age where I had to occasionally stumble into their bedrooms at three in the morning to rip soggy, pee-soaked sheets off a bed; and soggy, pee-soaked pajamas off a soggy, pee-soaked kid; I was fairly confident I was done with that part of parenting and my days of dealing with these kinds of bodily fluids were long over. So when I woke up one morning to hear my husband say, "Michelle, I'm really embarrassed to tell you this, but I think I wet the bed," I was more than a little bit horrified. I mean, I wasn't really expecting to have to deal with a soggy, pee-soaked husband for at least another thirty years.

But I'm getting ahead of myself. The story actually started several hours earlier than his sheepish admission. Sometime in the middle of the night he'd awoken to the very definite smell of pee. Strong pee. Frat-boy pee. Making the logical deduction that it was *his* pee, he handled it how most men in this middle-of-the-night situation handle it; Change the sheets? Dry the mattress? Nope. He stumbled to his pajama drawer to change his sleep shorts and grabbed a towel to put under his butt and went right back to sleep. Obviously.

Several hours later, he awoke to the sound of his alarm, and the smell of pee. This, coupled with the folded towel bunched up under his ass reminded him of the events in the middle of the night: the *peeing*. Since his brain was much clearer at dawn than it had been a few hours before, he frantically jumped out of bed and started patting his shorts. Bone dry. Sheets? Dry. However, the fact that he smelled like a petting zoo prompted him to continue his frenzied investigating — the mad patting which was alternated with him pressing his nose to the sheets and inhaling audibly: *so* audibly it woke me up.

**Me:** What the hell are you doing?

**Husband:** Michelle, I'm really embarrassed to tell you this, but I think I wet the bed.

Now, you should know that we have a king sized bed and sleep about a foot apart from each other so the fact that I did not instantly leap into a standing position when he said this shouldn't be puzzling. I wasn't worried about getting wet; I was more entertained by his frantic patting and sniffing and I'll admit, slightly amused (and alarmed) by the fact that my forty-four-year-old husband had wet the bed to do anything other than lay there and give him my best WTF look.

**Me:** Wait. What do you mean you wet the bed? Are the sheets wet? (I was assuming, hell, I was *praying*, that they were *not* due to the way his nose was pressed against them.)

**Husband:** No.

**Me:** Are your sleep shorts wet?

**Husband:** No, but they reek of pee. Here, smell them.

Have you ever had someone ask you to taste the milk to "see if it tastes funny" right after they spit it out into the sink? Exactly.

**Me:** I'm good. Gonna trust you on this one.

**Husband:** Smell the sheets, then.

**Me:** Seriously dude, not necessary. Are they wet?

**Husband:** No.

**Me (inwardly exhaling and canceling plans to Google "home health care nurse" and make a trip to the mattress store to purchase two twin beds later in the day):** Then I'm just going to go out on a limb here and assume YOU DID NOT WET THE BED.

He began to panic — to question his health — followed closely by his sobriety.

**Husband:** Do you think I have a bladder infection?

**Me:** Again, dry shorts, dry sheets — you *did not* pee yourself. Impossible.

**Husband:** Do you think I *blacked out* and peed myself?

Huh. Fair point. He *had* been experiencing a lot of stress at work and *had* been on quite a Jägermeister bender of late [and by *bender* I

I Just Want to Be Alone

mean he'd been enjoying sipping a shot (or two) of Jäger with a beer (or two) every night for the past week (or two)]. Nowhere near the "bender" stage, but hey, when you wake up to your sleep shorts reeking of piss it can make a man start to worry.

He immediately began an investigation. Went into the bathroom. Stripped down. Was in there for at least five minutes and I suspect was doing his damnedest to try to smell his junk, but I can't say for sure. Next he went downstairs to the bar to check the level of the Jägermeister bottle. Ignoring the fact that the level wasn't alarmingly low he decided he was most likely (definitely) an alcoholic. That realization coupled with his self-diagnosis of a rare illness in which the initial symptom was an uncontrollable bladder that produced pee that instantly dried made him panic.

**H:** I'm making a doctor's appointment.

It's probably a good time to tell you that this rash behavior of his isn't odd. Some people call him a germaphobe, but if they could see his bathroom sink, the inside of his car or his closet they'd quickly rethink that designation. Some may call him a hypochondriac, but the fact that he rarely gets sick disputes that. Is he pathophobic, suffering from a fear of disease? Maybe, but really, aren't we all? No, I believe he simply suffers from *Idon'twanttoshitmypantsinpublicaphobia*: the fear of LOSING ALL CONTROL OF BODILY FUNCTIONS. Let me tell you another story that might make his behavior make a little bit more sense.

Last month we went to our cabin, where we hadn't been in over six weeks. About ten minutes after we arrived my husband went into the bathroom. He immediately yelled, "Has anyone used the toilet since we got here?" We all replied that no, none of us had.

"Why?" I asked.

"Because there's a worm in the toilet and I was wondering whose ass it came out of."

We all rushed in to see, and indeed there was a worm — the kind you'd use to bait a fishing hook — covered in brown goop and slowly wriggling around on the bottom of the toilet bowl. After about three minutes of intensely staring at the worm, my husband stood up with a definite look of distress on his face.

"What's wrong?" I asked.

"I'm just wondering if maybe the last time I was here I took a shit right before I left and had something weird going on in my stomach."

He was dead serious.

He thought he pooped a worm.

*Six weeks ago.*

And also? IT WAS AN EARTHWORM.

But of course, he Googled it. The good news is that it's highly unlikely that the worm came out of his ass. The bad news is that it's very likely we have a crack in our pipe that allowed the worm to squeeze in and swim in our toilet.

So him jumping to conclusions about the fact (or the theory) that he'd wet the bed wasn't really that unusual.

Still asking me to smell his shorts, and with me still refusing, he stripped the bed and began smelling the mattress. He was clearly distressed. And I'll admit, by this time, so was I. Despite the fact that the sheets and mattress were dry, I was inwardly panicky (but outwardly sympathetic). While I was trying my best to reassure him THAT HE DID NOT WET THE BED I was having visions of plastic sheets and bedpans and began to imagine my life on fast forward:

Peeing the bed at forty-four.

Wiping his ass by fifty-five.

Changing his diaper by sixty.

Finding a super hot male nurse to help me out by sixty-one.

While the last task didn't sound *horrible*, this really wasn't in my plan. I'd always envisioned us growing older and enjoying the finer things in life, like dry underwear and sheets.

After a stressful day of worrying and Googling and self-diagnosing, and a beer and Jäger free evening, he went to grab a pair of sleep shorts out of his pajama drawer later that night.

They *reeked* of pee.

## I Just Want to Be Alone

He started furiously grabbing pairs of sleep shorts out of the drawer and pressing them to his face.

Pee. Pee. Pee.

All dry. All reeking of pee.

*Cat* pee.

And instantly he remembered how a few days before, our little cat, Lucy, had been trapped in his pajama drawer for hours after she'd crawled in and made a cozy bed for herself. I'm not sure how we'd missed the smell when we'd discovered her there or why we hadn't thought to check the drawer that morning, but the mystery was solved. He was so happy that he wasn't crazy, dying from bladder failure, or a raging alcoholic that Lucy didn't even get in trouble. And *I* was so happy that my (near) future was free of plastic sheets that I didn't even say, "I told you so."

And then we celebrated with a beer ... and a shot of Jäger.

*MICHELLE NEWMAN is the creator/head writer/only writer at You're My Favorite Today, a blog about her long suffering family, the absurdity of celebrity life (which she's absurdly addicted to) and anything else she can find hidden humor in. She is an* Entertainment Weekly *Community Contributor where she writes about and recaps some of her favorite television shows, and her writing has been included in the best selling humor anthology,* I Just Want To Pee Alone, *as well as on various websites such as Mamapedia and In The Powder Room.*

*Michelle lives in Minnesota (constantly dreaming of warmer climates) with her hilarious and very tolerating husband (who has demanded many rewards for the submission of this story) and two lovely and abnormally well-adjusted teenage daughters. And so far — thankfully — dry sheets.*

*Follow along @urmyfavetoday and connect on Facebook at You're My Favorite Today.*

# Somewhat Indecent Proposals
## By Ellen Williams and Erin Dymowski
### *Sisterhood of the Sensible Moms*

Ah, marriage. We are two friends, Ellen and Erin, who each have roughly twenty years in the marriage bank with our respective spouses. We are primed for a stroll down memory lane. Care to join us? Let's rephrase that, because we were just being polite: put on those running shoes, girl.

In fact, lace up for a major hike down that road. We're trekking to what comes before the "I dos" and the Polish dollar dances. Think further back than the marriage license. Think before the tortured nights you suffered deciding whether to have the duck l'orange or the orange roughy at your reception. (Damn you, Aunt Marge, and your seafood allergy.) Think back to where it all began.

Love and marriage may go together like a horse and carriage, but every bride-to-be worth her garter belt will tell you that at least in the beginning, it's all about the proposal. You need a proposal to kick this whole marriage roller coaster careening into motion. And you really need a great story to go along with that ring because otherwise, you might bore your bridal shower guests to the brink of comas. Seriously, they're trapped watching you open twenty-five individually gift wrapped shrimp forks. They deserve better.

Lucky for you, we have stories that are at least more riveting than Aunt Marge's bunions. Because bunions.

**Erin:** Ellen and I were both in our early twenties when we got married to our men. Young adults ready to take …

**Ellen:** Oh, who are you kidding? Through our forty-ish-year-old lenses, we look like embryos. Frank and I met in our junior year of college, a time when beer was a priority and a box of pasta was a week's worth of groceries. Dinner out was the Chinese place next to the frat house because the price was right; rumors of cat meat be damned.

**Erin:** Steve and I weren't much better. We would hoard our "extra" laundry quarters for a hot Saturday morning date at the bagel place.

**Ellen:** Mmmm, dirty socks and lox.

# I Just Want to Be Alone

**Erin:** It was slim pickins all around. Starving students and all that.

**Ellen:** We were so student-poor that riding in a limousine was our running, wistful joke. Whenever a stretch with tinted windows would pass, Frank would say, "There's our limo." My standard reply was an eye roll so epic, every tween girl within a twenty mile radius would fall to her knees to worship me. The joke was really on me because stumbling up the steps of the shuttle bus is hard when you're scanning your own cerebellum.

**Erin:** Ah, young love and public transportation, but your college romance continued even after keg stands were a distant memory.

**Ellen:** A distant memory for one of us. I was in Baltimore being slammed by medical school and my row house's ancient plumbing – longing for the lazy days of college and hot showers. Frank was living over an hour away working hard, banking some coin at his family's business, but still kicking it college-party-style living in a hygienically challenged apartment with a roommate. What he lacked in nostalgia, he made up for with regret every morning when that alarm clock blared.

**Erin:** I feel like you're about to segue into bunions. Where's the proposal?

**Ellen:** I'm setting the scene for THE DAY. We were celebrating. I just didn't know we would be celebrating our engagement. We had been together for two years and Frank had scraped together enough money to pay for a dinner that didn't meow. I was even told to wear a skirt and heels to his apartment. However, when he said, "There's our limo," I just continued walking to the car. Only this time it *was* our limo and it was a very special one indeed because it was driven by Charlie. And Charlie was a local.

**Erin:** Wait a minute. This happened in our current place of residence, Bucolic County, USA?

**Ellen:** Yep.

**Erin:** The place where we have chosen to make our lives, but where certain natives have a certain kind of charm? The kind of charm where phrases like "I'm wearing my good camo to Grandma's funeral" get flung around like buckshot on the first day of deer season?

**Ellen:** Yep. Our driver, Charlie, was exactly this brand of charmer. A disregard for sunscreen and a love for cigarettes put his age somewhere between forty-five and sixty-seven. His suit was more shrink wrap than uniform.

**Erin:** He had a wad of chaw in his cheek, didn't he?

**Ellen:** He wasn't that unprofessional ... yet. Although, our down-home adventure did begin with Charlie greeting us, clapping Frank on the back, and then plopping into the driver's seat. Charlie immediately realized he had forgotten something – popping the locks.

**Erin:** Well, Frank was there to get the door for you, Diva. Pretty sure your arms weren't broken either, just sayin'.

**Ellen:** But this was the limo dream, and there were expectations. Anyway, Charlie was pretty intent on showing us all of the features of the limo. Too bad it was at sixty miles per hour with his head swiveled around for direct eye contact. His two-handed gesturing was worthy of a maestro. But I really shouldn't complain. He casually turned his attention to the road just as we were merging across four lanes of I-95 on our way to Philadelphia. He even let us show off our new trick of raising the partition. The first of many times that partition would need to be raised. Like I said, Charlie liked direct eye contact.

**Erin:** That Charlie, professional *and* considerate. Who needed privacy from someone like him?

**Ellen:** Forty minutes and a half a bottle of champagne later, Charlie pulled into the parking lot of Veteran's Stadium.

**Erin:** Was this one of those remote romantic set-ups? Were there violins and rose petals?

**Ellen:** No. There was Charlie bending over the engine with his chauffeur crack showing muttering, "I think we're overheating."

Frank muttered, "Aren't there gauges for that?" while I added a sardonic, "There's no steam." But as I mentioned before, our man was a professional and he tinkered and banged until he was sure and Frank was in a sweat worrying we would be late.

**Erin:** Frank had to be dissolving into a puddle! He was going to PROPOSE. Couldn't you see him jittering?

**Ellen:** Well thankfully, just at that moment, Charlie slammed the hood and we were on our way. For a full three minutes. *Whiiiiir-rrrrrrr* went the partition and Charlie asked, "Do you know where the restaurant is?"

**Erin:** Now Frank had to be losing it.

**Ellen:** More than kind of. This was before GPS or smartphones.

**Erin:** This was 1992, right? Cell phones were mini-suitcases that required choices like, "Do I want to pay the rent or do I really need to call 911?"

**Ellen:** Frank growled, "Find it," and our captain went into what an optimist would call action. Charlie raised and lowered the partition with strobe light frequency treating us to a peepshow of flying maps and muttered curses. It was so thoughtful to keep us apprised of just how lost he was. And oh yes, there were stops at street corners to ask for directions.

**Erin:** This was Philly. There aren't too many Boy Scouts hanging out on those corners.

**Ellen:** We were lucky to make it to the restaurant with our hub-caps and our wallets. But we did, and we had a lovely time with even more wine. Charlie even remembered to pick us up.

**Erin:** Never underestimate the power of a tip to get even the sorriest of asses in gear.

**Ellen:** Ah, but my night was not over. Frank was asking for my hand in marriage and darn it, he was doing it on the way home in the limo because he knew I hated public spectacles. Although, I still suspect he was hoping for some private display of amorous glee.

**Erin:** Frank should give lessons on how to construct a classy cover story.

**Ellen:** And that is where the classy ends. Moments after I said yes to the ring – not to the act of amorous glee – *whiiiiirrrrrrrr* went the partition. Charlie announced, "I gotta take a whizz."

**Erin:** Oh, the timing! You've got to admire him just a little bit. That's more than a gift; it's practically an art form.

**Ellen:** You can love on this Leonardo of the Limousine Industry later, because it gets better, or maybe I mean worse. With astute Charlie-esque intuition, he pulls into a crummy gas station with a tiny bullet-proof cashier cubicle . . . and no bathroom. But when you're Charlie, the world is your urinal, including the edge of the parking lot five feet from our window.

**Erin:** Well at least someone's little man gotten taken out to play.

**Ellen:** Wait. You let me get through this entire story. You usually suffer from *Ellen Interruptus*.

**Erin:** Well, if your engagement story was *Pretty Woman* meets *Animal House* . . .

**Ellen**: Did you just call me a hooker?

**Erin:** It was more of a limo reference. Anyway, my story was more *Three's Company* meets *Every Romantic Comedy Ever*. See, Steve basically couldn't even talk to me once he decided to pop the question. Like at all, and we were living two hours apart pre-cellphone or check-in texting. I became a little crazy in my week-long cone of silence. I was convinced we could not handle the long distance thing, and we were over.

**Ellen:** Touched by a bit of melodrama? Channeling *90210*?

**Erin:** By the time he came to pick me up for the weekend I was sure we were through and I told him so. I led off with, "I don't think this is going to work." He basically chucked the ring box at my head.

**Ellen:** Hmph. Don't take this the wrong way, but I think you could have used a little Charlie in your life.

**Erin:** And how could THAT be taken the wrong way?

Here's to twenty-plus year marriages no matter how you get to them.

## I Just Want to Be Alone

*ELLEN WILLIAMS and ERIN DYMOWSKI are the dynamic freelance writing duo proving that sensible and funny are not mutually exclusive on their shared award-winning blog,* Sisterhood of the Sensible Moms. *BUT they don't share everything: Erin has 5 kids with her husband Steve and Ellen has two daughters with her husband Frank. They've got parenting covered from kindergarten to high school. Their blog is like a good Girls' Night Out conversation: full of stories, parenting advice, book and travel recommendations, and recipes. It's dosed heavily with humor with a dash of snark, but softened with a sprinkling of sweetness. They are Pinterest Ninjas, carpoolers extraordinaire, and Nikon warriors. In addition, they are BlogHer Humor Voices of the Year and co-authors of the anthology* "You Have Lipstick On Your Teeth" *and can be found on Mamapedia, BonBon Break, In the Powder Room, and* The Huffington Post. *Connect with them on* Facebook, Pinterest, Instagram, *and* Twitter.

# Mr. Sensitive
## by Kristen
### *Life On Peanut Layne*

You've probably heard the phrase "open mouth, insert foot" before, right? Most of us have even been guilty of doing it ourselves. For example, you get stuck talking to someone you don't know very well at the playground and you're struggling to keep up with an already awkward conversation. Without thinking you casually say something like "Wow, look at that bratty kid over there pushing all the kids off of the monkey bars. Where the hell are his parents and why aren't they stopping the little jerk-wad?"

To your horror they reply back with, "Um, that's my son." You quickly apologize and then run away as fast as you can because A) you're completely humiliated and B) you want to escape before they can follow you home and egg your house.

Fortunately for the majority of us, this kind of insert foot in mouth disease doesn't happen all that often. But for some people they have their foot so permanently stuck inside of their mouth, that they might as well make some orthodontic braces out of that shit.

In my opinion, there are two kinds of foot stickers in this world. There are those who thrive on being a rude, insensitive jerk-weed (otherwise known as single and staying that way), and then there are those who seem to be absolutely clueless whenever they say something offensive or hurtful. What makes me an expert on this? You'll see.

We recently brought home a puppy that we adore. She is the main topic of a lot of our conversations these days, whether people want to hear about her or not. My husband's sister and her family visited us for Thanksgiving and we were sitting around the table chatting about life with our new dog. We were explaining the reasons why we chose to get our dog from a breeder versus a rescue because the list of qualifications you had to meet to get a rescue dog were much too long and strict, and well, basically we just wanted to get a puppy before the age of eighty. My husband suddenly blurted out, "I don't understand that. You'd think that these rescue places would be thrilled that somebody actually wanted to adopt their dog. I mean it's basically a USED dog."

That's my husband. Otherwise known as Mr. Sensitive. Sorry, ladies and gents, he's taken.

One time while venting to him about a frustrating conversation I had with a friend who only has one child and was giving me parenting advice that wasn't very helpful to someone like myself with five kids, Mr. Sensitive's response was, "Wait, so you mean to tell me that they only have one kid? ONE KID? That's not parenting, that's called, oops you just had sex a little too hard."

Admit it, you're secretly falling in love with him, aren't you?

I recently gained a lot of weight thanks to a bad reaction to a birth control shot. There is nothing worse than having to go shopping to buy new clothes because you gained weight (pregnancy doesn't count). We were in the dressing room at a popular department store, while I was attempting to stuff my stretched marked to hell sausage rolls into skinny jeans that looked like they were made specifically for the Olsen twins. I was already bordering on the brink of a psychotic breakdown when Mr. Sensitive loudly suggested that I try shopping at one of those fat lady stores. I wasn't sure whether to cry, or beat him senseless with a plastic hanger. I briefly pictured myself on an episode of Snapped, with crime scene tape plastered all over the outside of the fitting rooms as detectives discussed the brutal hanger beating that led to this poor man's demise. All I needed was a jury of twelve obese housewives and I'd be golden. Rest in peace, motherfucker!

Before you think that my husband is a total douchebag who doesn't have a romantic bone in his body, think again. He does romance real good. One night while sitting on the couch watching television, he suddenly shouted at the top of his lungs "Get up, hold your breath, and RUN." Sometimes he's deep and philosophical too. Like when he asked me if I thought the song "Smelly Cat" from *Friends* was really about a cat with an odor problem, or rather was it code for a woman with a stinky vagina?

Speaking of vaginas, the most recent foot sticker/jackassery incident happened during a private, intimate moment between the two of us. Mr. Sensitive loves to talk dirty during sex. I'm not sure why, but once he gets going he just won't shut up. So there we were in the middle of doing the nasty (not sure what all the cool, hipsters are calling it these days but whatever), when he whispers this sweet little nothing into my ear:

**HIM:** I really like that you've gained so much weight because now your vagina is so much meatier.

**ME:** (Long pause) Wait, did you just call my vagina meaty?

**HIM:** Yeah, I guess I did.

**ME:** Babe, please do me a favor and don't try to talk sexy to me EVER again. What the hell?

**HIM:** Sorry, that didn't come out very good, did it?

**ME:** Not really. Ragu is meaty. Chili is meaty. But my vagina? Yeah, not so much.

Once the initial shock wore off, we both shared a pretty good laugh over that one. Our intimate moment was definitely ruined, but my meaty vagina is now a running joke between us. I still don't know whether to laugh or vomit whenever I find myself walking down the pasta aisle at the supermarket.

Despite Mr. Sensitive's knack for speaking in the native tongue that is also known as verbal diarrhea, he really is an amazing father and husband. Luckily so far none of our kids seemed to have inherited his uncanny ability to say all of the right words. Although, maybe that's not true, because there was that one time at a McDonald's drive thru when our older daughter told the cashier, "You're really pretty, but you're wearing way too much make-up."

When you think about it, there is something admirable about a person who isn't afraid to speak their mind. That's just one of the many things that I love about Mr. Sensitive, even if it also happens to drive me crazy. He isn't the type to sugar coat anything and will give me honest answers to my questions, even if I don't always want to hear them. I know if I ask him, "Do these jeans make my butt look big?" there is a good probability he'll answer back with, "Yes, and you're so buying them."

## I Just Want to Be Alone

*KRISTEN is an average mom to five super kids living in Portland, OR. She is a humorist blogger at Life On Peanut Layne, which promises to provide laughter, entertainment, and permanent birth control to the entire neighborhood. She is a contributing author in the best selling humor book* I Just Want to Pee Alone *and the e-book series* Life Well Blogged. *She is also a parent blogger for Families in the Loop. Kristen can be found on Facebook or Twitter when avoiding housework, so chances are high that you'll run into her.*

# Exploding With Love, Literally
## By Karen Alpert
### *Baby Sideburns*

The other night the hubby and I were lying (laying???) in bed and had the following conversation:

**ME:** Hey honey. So my friend is putting together this book, and we're supposed to write funny stories about our spouses, but I've been wracking my brain, and I can't think of a thing. I mean you're like really funny but for some reason I can't think of a funny *story* about you.

**GREG:** I have one.

**ME:** Really? You do?

Part of me was like super excited and relieved, but the other part of me was like, *Really, do you have one? Because I hope you're not just gonna tell me some stupid story about that time you and your friends did something stupid together.*

**GREG:** Remember the first time I met your mom?

*OK, this could be interesting. And scary.*

**ME:** Yeah?

**GREG:** Remember how I left so quickly?

**ME:** Uh-huh.

**GREG:** I never told you the reason.

**ME:** Yeah you did. You said your stomach hurt.

**GREG:** I mean I never told you the REAL reason.

*Ruh-roh.*

And then he proceeded to tell me a story that I can't F'ing believe he held in for eight years.

It was 2006 (holy crap, that sounds sooo dated now). Greg and I had been dating for a few months and my mom was coming to town to visit. Awwww shit, time to ask him if he wants to start meeting my family.

**ME:** Heyyy, do you maybe want to go to dinner and meet my mom or would you rather dump me?

Because I was almost thirty-five, I had done this shit enough times to know that a guy will only shoot the shit with relatives if he likes you. Like if he REALLY likes you. Not like if he just REALLY likes your vajayjay.

**GREG:** Sure. That'd be cool.

Holy crap, this guy is serious! He really likes me. Shit, what's wrong with him?

Anyways, as my mom's visit neared I made reservations at a nice restaurant called Expensivo (not really, but this was at a time in my life when I was a young jackass who intentionally picked the most expensive restaurants I could find when my parents were coming to town because I knew they'd pay). I can barely remember the meal except that Greg had this awesome French onion soup and he and my mom are both talkers so there weren't any awkward silences as far as I can remember. And then after dinner we walked home until this happened.

**GREG (YELLING):** OKAY, IT WAS GREAT MEETING YOU, ROBERTA! GOODNIGHT!!

Wait, what? We were still like fifty yards from my place. And why was he yelling at us?

So here's why. Wait, I just want to pause for a moment here and tell my mom something. Mom, I'm sure you're reading this so I wanted to say you might want to stop here. Oh, and Grandma, you too. And anyone else I'm related to. OK, so to everyone except for my mom and my grandma and everyone else in our family, here's why he was yelling.

He shat himself.

I shit you not. No, not like he sharted (and if you don't know what sharted means, go look it up because I'm too lazy to explain it). His stomach was totally upset and he full-on shat himself right there on the corner of my block. He felt it coming so he started talking REALLY LOUDLY to hide the sound of it.

*Squirrrrrrrrrrrrrrrrrttttttttt* is what we should have heard, but instead all we heard was him screaming, "IT WAS GREAT MEETING YOU, ROBERTA! GOODNIGHT!!"

And it was so bad that as he was running to his car, IT was running down his leg. *Ewwwwwwwwwww* (I cannot push the "w" key enough times).

So while my mom and I were trying *not* to discuss the awkward goodbye and how he clearly didn't like her and was going to break up with me, guess what he was doing? He was in the alley stripping down and getting butt-naked (or is it buck-naked??? I can never remember, but it should be butt). And then he threw his gross poopie pants into the darkness because hell if he was gonna bring all that nasty stank into his car. But of course he couldn't drive home bottomless. What if it happened again? Because you know, shit happens. Especially "explosive, upset-stomach because you're meeting your girlfriend's mother for the first time" kind of shit.

Well, thank God there was a towel in his car, so he did what any normal human being would do. He fashioned it into a huge diaper and wore it home. Can't you just picture a grown man wearing a giant towel diaper?

Just to paint you a picture, imagine a super skinny, tall, practically Albino Sumo wrestler. I don't know about you, but I would have paid good money (not much because I'm kinda cheap) to see him get pulled over by a cop wearing this. But alas, he didn't break any laws that night. Wait, yes he did. A bunch. But there were no driving infractions.

Oh, and to make matters worse (which pretty much seems impossible at this point), he had a female roommate and he totally had to sneak into his apartment all stealthily and shit so she wouldn't see him wearing this ginormous towel diaper. Bwhahahahahaha! Uhhh, I mean I feel so bad for him.

**GREG:** So that's what really happened that night.

**ME:** Can't. Breathe. Laughing. Too. Hard.

Seriously, my pillow felt like it had gone through a carwash. I was laughing so F'ing hard I was sobbing as he told me this. So even though I can't think of a single other funny thing that has happened in the eight years we've been together, this is plenty. Plus, I love that my husband was SOOOOOO nervous about meeting my mother that he shat himself. That, my friends, is love.

## I Just Want to Be Alone

*When KAREN ALPERT isn't taking care of her rug rats (or when she's purposely ignoring them because they're being douchenuggets) she spends her time writing the popular blog <u>Baby Sideburns</u>. She's written a number of viral posts including What NOT to F'ing Buy My Kids This Holiday, Daddy Sticker Chart and What I Really F'ing Want for Mother's Day. In 2013 she self-published her first book, <u>I Heart My Little A-Holes</u>, which quickly became an Amazon best-seller and a New York Times Best-Seller, and will be re-released in April 2014 by HarperCollins. She is married to her awesome husband Greg and in case it isn't obvious, she also spends a lot of time putting money in her swear jar. Sorry, her F'ing swear jar.*

# And I Still Haven't Killed Him
## By Allison Hart
### *Motherhood, WTF?*

My husband is wonderful. He's wonderful at many things. Stress is not one of them. I'm not saying that I am a stress-master, but I'm a hell of a lot better at it than he is. For one thing, I do not become *Insane While Sleeping*. By contrast, *Insane While Sleeping (IWS™)* is his specialty.

The first time I encountered my husband's unique brand of unconscious lunacy was when he managed a juice bar back while we were still dating. Weeks of constant juice-making, the apparent stress of carrots, strawberries, and wheatgrass shots, triggered a brief bout of IWS. I lay fast asleep in that wonderful worry-free way that only a childless person can, when my husband suddenly spoke to me in a totally normal conversational tone:

"Allison ... Allison ... Hey, Allison."

"WHAT?"

"You've got to try this smoothie."

"What? What are you talking about?"

"This smoothie. You've got to try it. It's really good."

"What? What are you talking about?"

"The *smoothie*. You should try it. You'll love it."

Actually worried about what I had gotten myself into with this guy, I asked, "Are you a crazy person? Have you gone crazy?"

"What? Why? No."

"There is no smoothie."

"Yes there is."

"No there's not."

"Yes there is."

Seriously. We had this argument.

*And now I'm going to kill you, Husband.* "There is no fucking smoothie you weird crazy person."

"There is a smoothie and I'm not crazy."

"Fine! Give me the smoothie. *Show me your fucking smoothie.*"

"OK."

With that, he rolled over, ostensibly to reach off the edge of the bed to the floor where he kept his middle of the night delicious smoothies. What's more annoying than being woken up by this crazy nonsense? Having the person on the other side of the argument, upon realizing there was indeed no smoothie, simply go back to sleep. He rolled over, reached to the floor, and then just lay still. Blissfully asleep. It was over for him, while I lay beside him fuming.

Worse: In the morning? He didn't believe me.

As a lifelong insomniac, my sleep is fragile. Once awoken, I don't fall back to sleep. Like, at all. Ever. Luckily, the years brought on only a few additional episodes of IWS. I married him anyway. Then we had a baby and I slept almost never. In those early baby days I could count my nightly sleep hours on one Simpsons' hand and still have one or two digits to spare. Meanwhile, my husband slept every time his conscious presence was not actively needed.

Our baby didn't sleep in our room with us. We shared our room with him for half of his first night home, and then agreed to move him into his own room so we could sleep at least when he was sleeping. Even on that first half-night, the baby was not in our bed with us. To clarify: the baby didn't sleep in our room, and never once in all his life slept in our bed. (Don't judge me, co-sleepers; I don't judge you.) I tell you this so you can appreciate how very crazy what happens next was.

We were probably about three weeks into this sleepless (for me) journey down the rabbit hole of parenthood. I was dead asleep one night when I woke up to my husband digging through the sheets and blankets in a blind panic.

Alarmed and a little pissed, I asked, "What are you doing?"

"I can't find him!"

He crawled around bed, desperately feeling the blankets.

"Can't find who? What are you doing? What are you talking about?"

He was clearly unhinged. He practically shrieked, "The *baby*! I can't find the baby! *Help me find the baby!*"

"The baby isn't in the bed. The baby is in his room. What are you doing?"

Then I realized that my husband was smack-dab in the middle of an IWS attack, and I immediately understood that I was about to commit murder.

"You are sleeping! The baby is sleeping! I *WAS* SLEEPING! Are you freaking kidding me with this?"

With that, he lay down and went back to sleep. My heart raced as I thought through possible scenarios and everything I knew about the disposal of a body (nothing at all).

He did this nightly for awhile then tapered off to just a couple of times per week. I never did muster the energy to get up and kill the guy. But I like to think that the looks I gave him all day every day during those early days killed just a little part of him.

*ALLISON HART writes the humorous and (sometimes brutally) honest blog Motherhood, WTF? As the self-proclaimed "mom who makes you feel better about your parenting," she says the things that other moms have the good sense to only think.*

*Allison made her print debut in the much lauded and hilarious anthology* "You Have Lipstick on Your Teeth."

*When not banging her head against the wall and repeating herself to her children, she can be found making people feel better about their parenting all over the Internet. You can find her on her* blog, Facebook, Twitter, *and* Pinterest.

# My Obnoxiously Skinny Husband
## by Lynn Morrison
### *The Nomad Mom Diary*

The first time my mother met my husband, he was wearing a Speedo.

Arizona. It's one hundred and three degrees in the shade. My mother and sister are sipping poolside cocktails. I'm tugging on the back of my swimsuit, hopelessly trying to cover up my butt. My husband (boyfriend at the time) struts up in a blue Speedo. My mother looks like a deer caught in headlights, her thought bubble clearly screaming, "Don't look down! Don't look down!" My sister laughs so hard she spills her drink. Or maybe she peed from laughter. It's tough to tell. I'm busy looking for any escape that will bring an end to the conversation. I finally spy two free inner tubes and drag him off to round them up. As we walk away I hear my mother utter the eight words that could cause any woman to drink or put her head in the oven, "Good lord, his butt is smaller than hers."

My husband is obnoxiously skinny. He stopped gaining weight in '93. Yes, 1993. At fifteen years old he assumed his current form like some bizarre twiggy alien. It hasn't changed since. Adding insult to injury, he eats second helpings of dessert as if his life depends on it. Secretly, I keep hoping that someday all those second helpings will show up on his ass, but no luck so far. The more he eats, the thinner he gets. Worse, he does things like biking to and from work in the rain, sleet, and snow. He goes to the gym three times a week, by choice. The other day he managed to pinch a millimeter of skin on his belly and immediately dropped to the floor and started doing sit-ups.

On that warm Arizona afternoon, I make it my life's mission to make my mother eat her words. I may not have been born with my husband's metabolism, but I've got street smarts and moxie. If I can't get thin, I'll make him fat. If I have to feed the man whole milk by the gallon, I'll do it. Come hell or high water, thin man will gain weight. Or, at the very least his ass will.

In the early days of our relationship, I carefully studied his eating habits and made notes of any potential Achilles' heels. Chocolate? Yes. Whipped cream? Absolutely not. Piping hot apple cobbler? Hell yeah. I charted, compared, and experimented for months on end. By the time we got engaged, I was baking twice daily and could tell you how to double the fat and calorie content of any recipe, including a salad.

On the surface, it seemed to work. I baked. He ate. He ate firsts, seconds, and thirds. He ate all day long and finished everything that I carried from my oven to the kitchen table.

Again I charted and compared, chortling with glee every time I saw him reach for another spoonful of cobbler. I couldn't lose.

Turns out, I was fifty percent right. I couldn't lose. He could. That long and lanky figure failed to pack on a single ounce while my curvaceous backside began to rival a Kardashian in a swimsuit. Despite my attention to detail and careful planning, every cup of sugar resulted in one less ounce for him and one more pound for me. He ate, but I gained.

A few months into our marriage the situation finally came to a head: the first of what would be many, many conversations about my "health:"

"Have you put on weight?"

I'm carrying a handful of chocolate smeared plates to the kitchen sink. I nearly drop them as the words pierce through the sugar high. Have. You. Put. On. Weight. Question mark. The months of rage and frustration over my futile efforts burst forth into a string of vitriol that would shock Charlie Sheen on Twitter.

"HAVE I PUT ON WEIGHT?" I screech. "How have you NOT put on weight? I've slaved over this stove for hours, used real cream and butter, doubled the chocolate chips and bookmarked over a hundred recipes that have the word 'lard' in the title. I've done everything a girl can possibly do to change the marital male backside to female backside ratio in this house. What have YOU been doing?"

My husband doesn't miss a beat. "Exercising. Maybe you should try that instead." With those words my indignation and control over the situation fly out the window. I consider murdering him, but stop as the image of prison food leaps into my head.

It becomes my husband's turn to chart and compare. He chortles with glee each time my chair creaks underneath my sizable ass. Me, on the other hand, I absolutely loathe every conversation we have about weight. He asks me to join him at the gym. I lie, feigning a sprained ankle. I'll do almost anything to avoid conversations about my weight, but I draw the line at actual exercise. The worst part is that I can see them coming from a mile away: I bake, he loses a pound. My pants start to shrink around me. If I don't act fast, we're going to have to have the "are we still paying for your unused gym membership" talk.

If I put half the effort into exercising that I put into hiding the fact that I haven't been exercising, I wouldn't be in this situation in the first place. Unfortunately, all those years of being Betty Crocker had an impact. I can't stop baking. We can't stop eating. So I'm constantly searching for the secret to losing weight like he does, without having to spend all my time in the gym.

My quest has led me down paths I hope to never stumble along again. There was that horrid visit to the gym for a fat-measuring pinch test that would make a mammogram look like a breast massage. Anytime I get close to the gym I have flashbacks of the hairy man-hands fondling my fat rolls. Is it any wonder that I don't want to go?

Scarred for life, I decided that an impersonal online test might be a safer option. During one of my million Google searches for diet advice, I stumbled across a calculator that lets you put in your height and weight and then it tells you your body mass category: underweight, healthy, overweight or obese. I hovered over the keyboard as I entered my undeniable statistics… 5'10" and a hundred and something pounds. I typed it in and sat through a long delay.

I held my breath and prayed that the damn thing could somehow sense anxiety and would say, "You're perfect, don't change anything." *Voilà!* Not a moment too soon, the results screen came up and said I was "healthy." HEALTHY! I haven't been that excited since fifth grade when the cute boy almost remembered my name (Lisa… Lynn…close enough). Granted, I was less than two potato chips away from the overweight category, but my husband didn't have to know that.

I put down my chocolate chip cookie and put my offense into motion. "Look honey, my weight is absolutely normal for my height."

That was a big mistake. He hadn't yet noticed that my boob fat was hanging out the side of my nightgown. He hadn't until I invited him to take a closer look. He cast a critical eye in my direction and demanded that I rerun the test in front of him.

I debated telling him my statistics for about two seconds before realizing that righteous indignation was going to be a much better solution. "What do you mean 'rerun the test'? Don't you trust me? I can't be with someone who doesn't trust me! Maybe it is *you* that isn't trustworthy! What have you been up to? Is there something you're not telling me?!?!" He never asked about the test again.

My favorite was the time I put on his skinny ass jeans and managed to zip them up. "Oh, are those new jeans?" he asked me. "They're nice!"

"Yep, I just borrowed them from *your* closet."

He started shrieking for me to "STOP STRETCHING THEM" and then spent the rest of the evening running them through the washer and dryer to try and shrink them back again. I bought myself peace, quiet, and some deep personal satisfaction. *Take that, boney ass!*

Unfortunately, my ability to gloat ran out around the same time as my birth control prescription. Ah, pregnancy and the luxury of having a medical excuse to pack on the pounds! I waltzed into the eighth month check-up, hand-in-hand with my husband. We were going to discuss the birth plan. I completely forgot that at some point I'd have to be weighed. If I'd had anything in my hands, I'd have clubbed the nurse over the head with it when she announced that I'd put on a healthy thirty pounds with my first pregnancy.

I assured my husband that it was all baby/water/blood and that it had nothing to do with my second breakfast habit and would absolutely come off as soon as I had the baby. No one was more shocked than I was when I failed to leave the fat behind in the delivery room. I don't know what evil genius of a hospital administrator thought it would be a good idea to put a scale in the hallway of the post-natal ward, but I can almost guarantee it was a man.

Once they coaxed me out of the fetal position at the base of the scale, I soldiered on and thankfully lost most of the weight pretty quickly. (Holla to the breastfeeders!) However, those last five pounds were a bitch and a half. For many, five little post-pregnancy pounds would be nothing. For me, five pounds is the fine line between lying on the bed panting as I squeeze the zipper up on his jeans and tear-stained cheeks when I can't get them over my hips.

In desperation, I pushed my cheap stroller with its plastic wheels up and down the cobblestoned streets of our small town to the tune of a hundred or so miles in two months. Then the wet fall weather set in. With three pounds left to go (yes, three pounds – I was killing myself over three miserable pounds), I needed a miracle. Thank God for girlfriends. One of them clued me in to the local gym that offered a daycare service AND had a sauna. For a dollar fifty, I could drop off my kid for a couple of hours, lazily pedal through twenty minutes on the stationary bike and then spend the rest of the time in the sauna, the tanning bed, the shower, and then primping in front of the mirror. I didn't lose the weight, but I looked so much better with brushed hair that my husband completely overlooked the inch of muffin top around my jeans. Problem solved.

I live in fear of those women who bounce back from pregnancy more fit than they were before. I'd ask how they do it, but I'm sure I know…they eat right and work out like crazy, just like my husband. Obviously, I don't have time for that. For me, there is nothing worse than having my husband peek over my shoulder mid-Facebook newsfeed scroll and see six-pack abs on a woman cradling a new baby. I might as well hand him a soapbox and a megaphone. One day the infamous "What's your excuse" photo landed right above a shot of a friend of mine showing her CrossFit-ripped, Paleo-stripped mid-section. He lobbed the hand-grenade from across the room. "Is that Jess?" I closed the browser window faster than the time porn came up on my work computer. That episode sucked because I now have to hide in the bathroom and pre-scan my Facebook feed before I do a full read on the couch. Skinny bitches are really cutting into my celebrity trash magazine time.

Thankfully major incidents like these don't happen very often. But there's one thing that gets me every year. Like the sword of Damocles hanging over my head: Winter. Mother effer. When the leaves start to fall, my butt begins packing away resources for the long winter ahead. My ass knows it needs to gear up for many hours spent in uncomfortable chairs at the dinner table overindulging in holiday delights. I can't help it. It's built into my DNA. But while everyone else in the known universe is gaining alongside me, my husband, Skeletor, is somehow losing weight. How does he do that?

The long winter season and all of its holiday dinners call for the big guns – maternity pants and stomach flu. Maternity pants are the ideal winter-wear for any woman trying to hide a few pounds. I just roll those suckers right up over the bulging belly and the dreaded muffin top disappears. (Plus I am warm and toasty!) The only way I can get away with this little trick is to never, ever undress in front of my husband. I've been known to hide in the closet, put on my pajamas at six in the evening, and/or carry my clothes into the shower. I'll do whatever it takes to keep this my little secret.

Once the festive season and its endless parade of chocolates and cakes is past, I head on over to my local hole-in-the-wall, grade C- restaurant. There, I order one of everything with a side of secret sauce. That butter-laden cream sauce greases the way down for the e-coli casserole. The meal works its magic within twelve hours every single time. I spend a miserably productive next couple of days, but it is well worth the pain. The uninterrupted hours of reading time while I lay dying in the bathroom floor are an added bonus! I like to call it a lose-lose-win situation for all involved.

Unfortunately for me, my freakishly thin husband has caught on to most of my tricks. He expects to see signs of telltale soreness after a gym class. He pretends to grope me, but really he's checking my waistband. Not much gets past him. Fortunately, he has left me one thing. Last year I lost twelve pounds before the doctor finally diagnosed and cured my incredibly brutal and effective foreign stomach bacterial infection (if I can ever figure out where I got it in the first place, I'll definitely bottle that stuff and sell it). I'd just enjoyed my first real dinner in a month when my husband looked at me from across the table and said, "Don't undo the good the diarrhea has done."

It has been ten years since that first fateful meeting between my husband's porn star swimsuit and my mother. Ten long years of struggling to make my thirty two inch hips fit into his thirty one inch waistline. The other day he eyed me as I got up from the table and re-peated the words that long ago set me off. "Have you put on weight?" As I struggled to find the fire and brimstone response of yesteryear, he added a new line and derailed my mounting rage. "I don't care if you have gained. I just want you here and healthy for a long, long time."

It turns out that all this time I've been focused on what's be-hind us, he's been thinking about what is yet to come.

*LYNN MORRISON is a smart-ass American raising two prim princesses with her obnoxiously skinny Italian husband in Oxford, England. Born and raised in the Deep American South, Lynn avoided becoming mired in the Mississippi mud by escaping to go to college in California. Had she known that the move would eventually lead to marriage to a nerdy Italian, she might have chosen a mud mask instead. As the Nomad Mom, Lynn exposes the truth about what it's like to be married to an uber-brainiac and the mother to multilingual children. The truth is, her days are pretty much like everyone else's, just with more pronunciations of the word "water."*

*After a long day of struggling to remember to say "chap" instead of "y'all" or "dude," Lynn likes nothing better than to curl up with her Macbook and a glass of wine and write thought-provoking essays on why sweatpants are the new black or why it is impossible to suck it in for eight hours. If you've ever hidden pizza boxes at the bottom of the trash or worn maternity pants when not pregnant, chances are you'll like the Nomad Mom Diary. You can also find Lynn over on BLUNTmoms.com, The Huffington Post, and Parentdish Canada.*

# The PerfectMan.com
## By Stacey Hatton
### *Nurse Mommy Laughs*

There was a brief time in my single life, when I wasn't dating.

OK, it was ten years…but I was busy!

Finally, when I had my work life in order, felt healthy and fit, and built up some confidence with my friend, Pinot, of the prestigious Noir family; I realized I had been ignoring the ticking of my biological clock.

It was time for me to jump back on the horse. So to speak…

Some of my single friends had had luck with Internet dating and at the time, it was new and the popular way to lasso a good man. This method of screening someone behind your screen sounded "analytically" appropriate. I figured since I was looking for someone with that part of their brain highly functioning, there could be an inordinate amount of them at my fingertips.

However, meeting these strangers was going to be a problem for my over imaginative brain:

*What if I find a guy I'm interested in, and then when we meet, I see he has forgotten to tell me he has a goiter the size of Detroit?*

*What if he's charming on the computer and phone -- but when we get together, I discover he's texting under the table his next guinea pig from the dating site?*

*OR, what if he smells like eggs?*

These were only a few of the crazy things that went through my mind. There was also the safety issue. Since I was living alone, I couldn't invite him to pick me up at my place. He could be a zombie locksmith and could come back to pick my locks. So to speak…

If I met him at a restaurant or bar, without anyone knowing my whereabouts, he could pull up in a white van with no rear windows – and I don't need to tell you what happens in those scenarios! You've seen *CSI*.

So when my best friend and I set up a fail proof strategy to watch my back – which was her being on speed-dial for the duration of the date -- I joined the dating site. I was impressed by how many questions you had to answer for the service I chose. If "the one" had the patience, intelligence and resolve to get through the question-naire, I might have pretty good luck meeting a winner.

Unfortunately, I didn't predict he might also have the personali-ty trait of *desperation*.

My first computer date was a handsome guy who said he was an actor. Don't groan! Growing up in the theater, I was flabbergasted to meet a straight actor who was interested in a commitment, so I had to meet him.

The minute we sat down, he told me what a talented actor he was, and that he just landed his first commercial role. Apparently, he had been a bartender or a fry chef at a hamburger chain since he graduated high school because he had no formal education and no other experience in acting. If he weren't so good looking, I would have reached across the table and bitch slapped that gorgeous chis-eled jaw line just to shut up his narcissistic babbling.

Needless to say, we did not find a love connection over an over-priced calzone, which I ended up paying for. Thank-you! NEXT!

By the time I met the following e-suitor, I had learned to ask more questions and spend time talking on the phone before meeting. He was an intellectual, who was arsty, funny, and appeared to be down-to-earth. This guy sounded like he had promise. After giving him the pre-trial run, he asked to meet him at a trendy, bourgeoisie type of restaurant which served Southeast Asian food.

When I walked in, I literally passed him twice because he didn't look anything like his picture. I don't even think it was a photo of his younger self, but an average looking guy in his college yearbook. This Mr. Potato Head was smart -- but quite shy at first. Thankfully, half way through our meal, he warmed up a bit and was able to ask me about which sex positions in the "Kama Sutra" I preferred. Check please!

Then there was the lovely man who talked about his ex-wife the entire meal. It would have been odd for him to do just that, but he was also well versed in name calling and trashing this poor woman. I was so happy his ex was able to get away from this moron; I wanted to ask for her address to send flowers with a congratulatory card.

*Nurse Mommy Laughs*

*Oh, for the love of increasing the population -- how am I going to ever want a second date, if all the men on this website are such LOSERS?!*

I began wondering if I should cancel my subscription to the dating site, and instead take up computer gambling. The odds were looking much better.

After walking away from it for a few months, I returned to the service and met a young guy whom I clicked with. We had similar interests; he had a wry sense of humor and a job. The first few dates were enjoyable. He didn't totally melt my socks, but he was a good guy, trustworthy and so much better than the others.

Much later, he invited me over for dinner at his place – an *apartment*. He seemed exceptionally old to still be paying rent, but maybe he had a logical reason. When I entered the apartment, I noticed he had the kitchen table set for two.

*Are those paper napkins or paper towels?*

*Give him a chance. What bachelor has real napkins?*

Then he asked me if I wanted a cocktail. That was going to be necessary to get over the voice in my head making fun of the folded paper towel I was later going to be placing in my lap. This true gentleman reached into a near empty fridge, brimming with Coors Light, and tossed me an unopened can with a smile.

*This dolt thinks giving me a Silver Bullet will metaphorically get me in the mood?*

Next, my knight-in-tarnishing-armor announced the menu, and thank goodness my robust ale didn't shoot out my nose.

Steak and lobster?! I couldn't believe it.

And I was further amazed by his manly skillz of fixin' steaks and lobster tails in a toaster oven perched atop the standard beige Formica countertops. The dude couldn't turn on the oven or fire up a grill?

Sorry Sir Lance-a-little, but Camelot this is not! Thou canst take thy rubbery lobster and joust it where the rising sun doesn't shine.

At this point, there were no more men I wanted to meet on the Internet.

Ever.

I canceled my service that night, while simultaneously popping

I Just Want to Be Alone

Tums in my mouth, like breath mints after a Caesar salad. No hard feelings, Computer – but you did me wrong.

Several months later at the hospital where I worked, I noticed some exotic-looking hotchilada, who periodically salsa'd to my floor. He always flashed his white, perfect smile, and laughed with his entire -- very firm -- body. At first I watched him from afar, but then I found ways to say something to him in passing.

*Was I feeling a connection from him too?!*

Finally, I got brave enough and asked one of his friends what his story was. "Señor Eye Candy" was single. His friend said we had to go on a date, probably because she was married and wanted to live vicariously through me, but I didn't mind being used in that manner.

Being the talented matchmaker that she was, she planned the entire date without me even having to ask him. I mean, who likes getting rejected in person? According to my friend, it didn't take much to talk him into the date. He had had his eye on me too, so we agreed to meet for a drink one night after work.

I was incredibly nervous as I entered the bar. I had driven past it many times, but had never stopped in. Getting there early, I reserved a table where I could see him come through the door. The waiting was excruciating, made me irrational … and have to pee.

*But I couldn't go to the bathroom or he might show up, see I'm not there and leave, or I could cut off the pee flow by crossing my legs, plus that might make my legs look longer and leaner. Good plan, Stacey. Good plan!*

Then the doors opened. It felt like slow motion. I was sure I was either going to pass out or hurl – but there he was. With the sun setting behind him, briefly blinding my view, I saw his silhouette inching toward the table. As my eyes adjusted to the light, I noticed him close – so close -- to our table, but he was looking around the bar over my head.

*He can't see me? Maybe the light messed with his eyes too.*

Next he tilted his head down toward me. I mustered up a tiny wave and a smile that caused me to blush, warming every cell down to my … toes. He was beautiful. My heart started to race.

Before I could say his name aloud, his smile jerked into a look of confusion. Moving a step back from the table, he asked, "Stacey?"

"Yes. I'm so glad you …"

"You're not her!" he loudly scoffed.

"Excuse me?" I whispered aghast. "I'm Stacey. Jenna set this up?"

Grabbing onto the back of the chair across from me, "You're not the girl I thought I was meeting."

*What the wha..? Am I being punked?* I thought while searching for hidden cameras.

"No. This won't do," he said, collapsing dramatically into the chair.

At this point, I was so stunned by his obnoxious behavior; I couldn't form any clear sentences or thoughts. I'm not sure why I didn't go off on him and tell him he was acting like an ass, but I truly think I may have been in medical shock.

After he explained to me that he had only agreed to go out with the "cute girl who had the daughter," it didn't take long for this nurse to figure out he wanted to bag my care assistant.

Since hindsight is 20/20 and I couldn't think rationally through my emotions, I asked if he wanted to stay. I should have stood up and left at this point, but my insecurities from enduring a year of awful Internet dating left me at a loss. "Mr. Gracious" said he would have one drink and then leave.

I don't remember much of that cocktail or what he said to me while I sat quietly, nodding like a bobble-headed mute. Of course, I do remember running to my car afterwards, spouting off fiery retorts which would have put him in his place.

As I tearfully drove home, I desired the comfort of my good friend, Pinot. But I knew this epic evening required an entire support team. So I pushed speed-dial for my best friend, and poured out the details of my horrific date.

Within thirty minutes, she appeared at my door with the perfect man of the night – Jose Cuervo. Because when you're dating, it's mandatory to have a fail-proof strategy to watch your back.

I Just Want to Be Alone

*STACEY HATTON is a former pediatric RN, mom of two girls, and humorist - hails from the laughter Mecca of the world, Kansas. You can find her musings on her blog,* <u>Nurse Mommy Laughs</u> *or her column in* The Kansas City Star *newspaper. She is an active member of the Erma Bombeck Writer's Workshop and the National Society of Newspaper Columnists. She is a contributing author in the books:* I Just Want to Pee Alone, Not Your Mother's Book...on Parenting, *and* My Funny Major Medical. *Her next project is co-creating the book* Not Your Mother's Book ... on Menopause *in between her mood swings, night sweats, and obsessive* <u>Facebook</u> *and* <u>Twitter</u> *habit.*

# The Case for the Bathroom Agreement
## By Meredith Napolitano
### *From Meredith to Mommy*

First comes love.

Then comes marriage.

Then comes acceptance of the whole crappy package.

You don't have to love every little snore, snort, toot, and belch that comes out of your man, but once you've committed to a lifetime, you better learn to accept them before you begin that lifetime of gritting your teeth and cracking a window.

With my hubby, I had to fall in love with him – and then learn to live with his bowels.

We all have bowels. We all have the need to empty them periodically. I grew up in a house with one bathroom. I get that the need to stink up the throne room can create some bathroom conflict. But you figure that everyone gets to lay claim to that sacred seat once a day. They do their darnedest to make sure they inconvenience the least amount of people when they do it, and they learn what Febreze does.

It turns out there's a difference between growing up in a house full of girls and marrying a man who has claimed pooping time as his favorite time of the day.

The signs were there when we met in college. I lived in a suite we four girls. We had two double rooms that shared a bathroom and common room. Our shared bathroom had a private stall with the seat of honor, and it was understood that if you locked the *stall*, but left the main door unlocked, it was safe to come in and shower, brush your teeth, curl your bangs (hey, it was the nineties), or whatever else girls do. If you locked the bathroom entirely, a deuce was in progress, and the ladies would give the room the space it needed. If you were planning on locking the door, you'd let people know with a simple "Hey, does anyone need anything in here before I lock the door?"

Message received. All the girls understood, all the girls complied. Just like I'd been raised.

Normal.

Sir Colon the Second lived next door to our suite in what was called an "adjoined single" – two single bedrooms sharing one bathroom in between with access from both sides. When we first started dating, we spent a lot of time hanging out in his room. He didn't seem to make frequent visits to the restroom – while we were in his room I probably visited it more than he did – but I *did* notice that he seemed to have a strange obsession with the toilet paper. He was concerned about how much of this precious commodity I was using during my visits, although gentlemanly enough to never actually request I bring my own. He was strangely focused on making sure there was always an ample supply at the ready. Once, when someone was, um, probably suffering from a weird stomach bug or food poisoning or whatever it is that afflicts college students around two in the morning, he *freaked out* when that someone attempted to wipe their mouth and the seat with TP. He pulled all his actual terrycloth towels down from the closet so that the Cottonelle stayed intact to be used only for its intended purpose.

That should have been my first clue.

When his parents came to visit, one of the jokes his mom made was about how much her grocery bill had gone down since she was no longer in charge of purchasing his TP stash. I thought it was *odd*, to make that sort of bathroom reference to your son's new girlfriend, but hey, everyone has their quirks. Maybe it was some sort of inside joke?

That should have been my second clue.

Then we graduated and moved out of the dorms, and started spending weekends at my apartment, and I noticed that he would make *several* long trips to the potty on Saturday or Sunday mornings, always with a magazine, maybe with an interesting book (smartphones were still a distant number two dream). We were getting more comfortable with our living habits, becoming a true couple, and I certainly didn't expect him to will his bowels into holding off simply because he was at his girlfriend's home.

But boy, that guy pooped a lot.

As we cruised into our permanent coupledom, I noticed that this man took his bathroom time *seriously*. We delayed many morning outings because he needed to drop the kids at the pool. Not once. Not twice. But sometimes *three* times. And *long* times. I just didn't get it.

We got married and moved into our first home. A home with not one, not two, but *three* bathrooms. We might have left the closing feeling a little house poor and like we didn't have a pot to piss in, but we were the proud owners of three to poop in.

And man, did he use them.

I would marvel at the fact that despite the fact that the toilets in our home outnumbered the humans living there, we still needed to clean *three* johns every week.

After a few years of married life, the man decided, while watching the news one night, that there were these super awesome cleansing regiments that jump started weight loss, and he was gung ho to try one. That month in our marriage I learned the true meaning of the term "oversharing" and what it means when you really *do* know far too much about your spouse. I also learned that I have no desire to ever try a cleanse, hear about a cleanse, or stand within five hundred feet of anyone participating in a cleanse.

Once those dark days had passed and I implored hubby dearest to put the mystery back in our marriage, we once again settled into what I had come to think of as "normal."

Then we had kids. Two of them in eighteen months.

And his bowels seemed to become, strangely, *more* active than before.

He'd say, "Go ahead, honey. Sleep in a little. I'll get up with the baby when she cries."

Baby cries for five, then ten minutes while I hide under my pillow. I finally give in and get up.

"Sorry, honey, she woke up when I was pooping!"

*Isn't that convenient?*

He'd exclaim, "Oh man, she definitely needs a new diaper. I'd do it, but she inspired me and now I have to poop!"

*Well, whaddaya know?*

I would leave him in charge and come home to a lame excuse like, "There's sort of a mess. I was watching them, but I had no IDEA they knew how to get into that closet! They did it while I was pooping."

*Fancy that.*

Every Sunday I was on my own. "I will totally help you get them ready for church. I'll get them dressed as soon as I'm done pooping."

*Shock and surprise – he missed his window.*

The man was taking long, leisurely restroom breaks, unbothered by our two needy babes, while I was squeezing my bowel movements into two minute increments when I thought something shiny might have captured their attention. I've had a two year old climb up onto my lap while I was doing my business without a care in the world, but his dump breaks remained relaxing and childfree.

I am SO STUPID.

Throughout our relationship, he'd established his routine, established this as his quirk, *just so* that when we had kids he would have a "get out of jail free" card! How could I possibly question him, how could I think he was shirking his fatherhood duties, when he had *always* been that way? That clever, clever, man. Amazing that a twenty-year-old college kid saw his college girlfriend and immediately thought ten to fifteen years into the future and began to lay the groundwork. Brilliant. This man was a psychic genius.

I mean, probably.

At any rate, once he had this lovely out, he also began some other frustrating behavior.

He refused to poop in any bathroom that contained a potty seat.

The potty seat in question didn't even have to be *on* the can. Its mere presence apparently established the room as a "kids' bathroom" where a grown man couldn't possibly enjoy a racing game on his smartphone with his pants down. He used to poop in the upstairs bathroom, but the girls took baths in that room, and he decided it wasn't "his" anymore.

And so he took his dominance into *my* bathroom.

The master bathroom – my oasis – became the *master's* bathroom. This wouldn't have been a big deal, if he didn't work from home. I stay at home. The kids are home. We are *all* home, *together,* all day long.

And now, not only is he noticeably absent when the girls get tough, he's using *our* bathroom to do it. The room where I keep my deodorant. The room where I keep my hairbrush. The room where I keep my toothbrush.

Time to throw my hair up in a ponytail and slap on some Lady Speed Stick before we dash out the door to library?

Oops! Daddy's in the bathroom.

Want to sneak in a shower before the girls wake up?

Sorry! Daddy's in the bathroom.

Was I hoping to brush my teeth before interacting with the moms in the carpool line?

Denied! Daddy's in the bathroom.

And my tolerance was *gone*. Flushed down the metaphorical toilet.

The time for a potty pre-nup had long passed, but as we approached our ten year anniversary, it was time for a new agreement. In the spirit of the *Big Bang Theory*, I thought through the circumstances thoroughly, drew it up, and presented it for him to sign. Preferably in blood.

### The Husband/Wife Bathroom Agreement

**Section 1: Exclusivity**
**Article 1: Morning**

1. Spouses agree that the master bathroom must remain open for usage by both parties between the hours of 6:00 AM and 9:00 AM. Open usage allows showering, grooming, and "number one" (although either party may request exclusivity for the purpose of "number one").

2. During these open use hours, one spouse may appeal for a ten (10) minute period of exclusivity. This appeal must include both a verbal notification that such a period is imminent, and a confirmed verbal positive response from the spouse being asked to relinquish access. This appeal will also require the pooping party to allow the

non-pooping party to gather necessary items from the room.

3. If the appeal for an exclusivity period is not granted, the spouse may choose another bathroom without commenting on the presence of Disney themed potty inserts. The spouse will not be required to use said inserts and is, in fact, discouraged to do so.

4. After the exclusivity period has ended, the pooping party is responsible for freshening the air, as well as warning the non-pooping party in the case where the air freshener has not performed up to standard.

5. In the event of a planned departure from the home, spouses agree to conclude all exclusivity periods fifteen (15) minutes prior to the agreed upon departure time.

## Article 2: Afternoon/Evening

1. Notification is no longer required for exclusivity periods of ten (10) minutes.

2. Any exclusivity period expected to be longer than ten (10) minutes requires notification.

## Section 2: Information

## Article 1: Oversharing

1. The only information about a poop that requires sharing is information that may need to be relayed to an emergency physician.

2. Any information that relates directly to what food may have been served by the spouse in a negative way allows the spouse to suspend food service until an appropriate apology has been granted.

## Section 3: Maintenance

## Article 1: Supplies

1. (S)he who uses up a supply shall replace it immediately.

2. Spouses are responsible for ensuring adequate supplies prior to a poop event. Should a pooping party fail to do this, the non-pooping party will have no obligation to procure and deliver said supplies.

## Article 2: Cleanliness

1. "Skid marks" in the bowl are never acceptable and will result in a loss of exclusivity privileges. The brush is right there.

2. "Seat splatter" is also unacceptable. See above. Clorox wipes

are right there as well.

3. The spouse who clocks the most time in the room takes responsibility for cleaning the room.

**Section 4: Childcare**

**Article 1: Avoidance**

1. A poop event is not a valid excuse for passing off childcare.

2. If a poop event by a child inspires a poop event by a parent, the parent is responsible for first cleaning any and all mess created by the child's poop event before beginning their own event.

3. Any misuse of poop events to avoid childcare will result in loss of master bathroom exclusivity.

Signed on this date

_____

Husband

_____

Wife

I love the man.

I love our marriage.

I love our babies in the baby carriage.

And if he adheres to the contract, I *might* just be able to accept his whole crappy package.

*MEREDITH NAPOLITANO is a former music teacher and choir director and current stay at home mom of two little girls, chronicling her balance between the roles of "Meredith" and "Mommy." With her stay at home life and a husband who works from a home office, she has family together time all day, every day! Meredith started blogging when she realized that she was spending far too much time on the phone with her best friend, sharing stories from life with two little ones, and it was time to give that poor woman a break and write these stories down. She blogs at* From Meredith to Mommy, *and spends her day searching for doll shoes, cleaning up messes, and escaping into social media.*

# The Day My Husband Saved My Ass
## By Heather Reese
### *My Husband Ate All My Ice Cream*

Anyone who's ever been pregnant knows that it's not all about newly glowing skin, rubbing your belly lovingly and wearing cute little maternity clothes. There's a dark side to pregnancy that many women don't talk about. It's the problems you get where the sun doesn't shine. The constipation, and the hemorrhoids. I was free and clear from the hemorrhoid issue in my first three pregnancies, but in my fourth, I had a rude introduction to that world.

Not only did I get my first hemmie, but it was the worst one ever. When it got to the point where I could no longer walk, sit, stand, sleep, or lay down, I was in so much pain that I decided I didn't care who I had to spread my cheeks for anymore. I needed professional help. The first doctor I went to said to try some Preparation H. So I waddled my way to the nearest pharmacy, paid for it, and unable to wait for relief, headed for the bathroom. I entered the stall and squatted, twisted, and turned, and finally applied the cream to the appropriate place. But instead of relief, I got intense burning. It felt like I'd applied Icy Hot to my bunghole. With my teeth gritted, I went home and hoped the relief would kick in. It didn't. My night consisted of me crying to my husband about my keister, laying in bed on my side, whining, and debating whether or not to risk the burning again and try more Preparation H. The next day I went back to the doctor, explained what happened and begged for some other form of relief. He asked to look at it again, so I dropped trou, and bared it all, again. This time he said it was thrombosed. For those lucky enough to not know what that means, basically, it meant that I had a blood clot in the tushie nugget. The only option? Surgery. But at that point, I didn't care. I wanted relief.

So the next day I went in for outpatient surgery. To spare you the details, it involved a very large needle full of numbing stuff that made me damn near jump off the table and bite the nurse's arm, and a very hot doctor. But I had relief, and that's all that mattered at that point. It took a whopping fifteen minutes, but it ended the excruciating pain I'd been in for days.

Three hemorrhoid-free years later, I found out I was pregnant again. Aside from the typical nausea, exhaustion, and back pain, things were going swimmingly until I hit twenty four weeks. And then ... I got constipated. I did everything they tell you do to in order to not get the wretched bum lumps. I drank tons of water, I didn't strain, and I upped my fiber. I did NOT want a dreaded repeat of the last hemorrhoid. But (no pun intended) during one fateful night in the bathroom, I wiped, and I felt it. The pain, burning, sharp needle, and awkwardness came back to me all at once. Immediately, I felt faint. My husband was already in bed, so I laid down and went to sleep, hoping it was all just a dream.

A few hours later, I woke up with pain radiating from my der-riere. I turned around in a panic, and shook Arick, trying to wake him up. He finally opened his eyes and immediately sat up, obvious-ly seeing that something was really wrong.

"What?" he said with confusion in his voice.

With tears in my eyes, and obviously slightly hormonal and irra-tional, I said, "I have another hemorrhoid ..."

He laid back down on the pillow and said, "I'm sure we have some more of that cream you used last time. Just go put that on."

My eyes were probably scorching a hole in his soul. "Oh ... you mean that DEVIL CREAM that BURNED MY ASS last time!? Yeah ... thanks a lot." I laid back down with my heart racing and tears in my eyes, afraid of the pain I was going to wake up to. With good reason. I woke up a few hours later, and it hurt to move. Until you have a hemorrhoid like that, you have no idea how many movements you make affect your general butthole area. Just to inform you, it's almost everything you do besides moving your head from side to side.

I didn't know what to do. Since I refused to use the devil cream again, Arick's solution was to go to the store and pick up something. But I didn't think I could manage the trip. And I didn't want to send him to pick out something for me. A few hours later though, after trying to wrangle kids and take care of, well, being alive, I was get-ting desperate. I thought that maybe since this one didn't feel thrombosed it might actually help enough to at least get me through going to the store to get something else. So, I went in the bathroom. I dug through the medicine closet, and found the tube and just stared at it for a few minutes, went to unbutton my pants, and threw the tube back in the closet and went to leave the bathroom.

*I'm just going to tough it out. I can make it through the store. It will be fine,* I thought.

But in the process of getting my shoes on, and trying to gather my things, I realized that I was oh-so-very wrong. Skittishly, I headed back into the bathroom, grabbed the tube again, and dropped my pants. I squirted some of the cream onto my finger, and delicately smeared it on, and that's when it started. The searing pain.

"OHHH MYYY GODDDD!!!" I yelled. I'm sure everyone in the house heard it. Tempted to put my ass in the toilet water to cool the burning, I stared at the tube. I turned it over and looked at the ingredients, convinced there was like, habanero pepper extract in it or something. Much to my surprise, there wasn't, but there was a vasoconstrictor. Yeah… that helps. Something that traps the BLOOD SUPPLY in the thing I'm trying to get to GO AWAY. No wonder I got a blood clot last time.

I pulled my pants up, got everybody loaded in the car and headed to the store, gritting my teeth and shifting uncomfortably the whole way. When we got there, I waddled my way to *that* aisle and surveyed my options. Anything with a vasoconstrictor was not an option. I grabbed a different kind of Preparation H, and noticed a spray that promised immediate relief. I was trying to debate on which one to get, and Arick told me to just get both. So I did. I was unsure about how I was going to aim the spray bottle, and keep it upright so that the bottle still sprayed appropriately, but I would cross that bridge later.

After grabbing a few more things, we checked out and headed to the car. I had the cream and the spray in my purse so that I didn't have to dig for them when we got home, and could go straight to the bathroom to use them. On the way home, I was reading the package for the spray and noticed in the directions it said the bottle would spray if it were held upside down, so that eliminated that problem and I knew I could do it without help.

I was so excited to be relieved, that I didn't even help Arick unload the car. I just walked straight into the bathroom as soon as we pulled into the driveway. Given my experience with Preparation H, I decided I'd try the spray first. I ripped the bottle out of the box and pulled down my pants. And then I was paralyzed by a fear that overcame the burning pain I was already in. When I hadn't come out of the bathroom a half an hour later, Arick asked, through the door, if I was okay. I pulled up my pants, opened the door, walked past him into our bedroom, and laid down. He followed me in there and asked what was wrong, and I told him I couldn't do it.

"Do you want me to do it for you?" I couldn't tell if he was serious. I just looked at him. "Give me the spray bottle and come here."

OMG. He was serious. At this point I wasn't sure what to do. Should I go in the bathroom, suck it up, and do it myself? Or drop my drawers and spread 'em for my husband? I reflected on the half hour I'd spent in the bathroom previously, and realized that there was no way I'd be able to do it myself because I was way too afraid of making it worse than it already was.

He was sitting on the edge of the bed. Like a kid about ready to get swatted with a belt, I got up, walked towards him, and pulled down my pants. We've been together for seven years. He's seen me give birth. I even pooped while I was pushing. Why was this such a big deal?

"I can't exactly squirt the bottle if I have to use my hands to spread your cheeks."

Oh. My. God. He seriously wants me to bend over and spread my own cheeks? I've seen this in porno movies. It doesn't end well. Again, I considered grabbing the bottle and heading for the bathroom, but I was frozen, just staring at him. Whether I was just stalling or honestly trying to think of another way for this to happen, I'm not even sure.

I slowly turned around so that my rear-end was facing him, and went to grab my own butt cheeks, and swiftly turned back around to face him. "I can't do it. It's going to be cold."

"I've been holding the bottle in my hand to warm it up. It will be fine. Turn around."

Damn it. I started to turn around again. "It's going to hurt!" I said, turning to face him again.

He started laughing and asked if I wanted to be in pain forever.

"Maybe I should try the new cream first. I mean, it has different ingredients, so it might not burn like the old stuff."

"HEATHER. Stop it. Just come here," he said, laughing.

"No ... just never mind. It's not that bad right now. I'll just deal with it. I think it's getting better." I lied, grabbing my pants to pull them back up. Somewhere on the Internet I had read that if I just stick a clove of garlic up my bunghole, it would cure the issue overnight. That was a much better option than this.

But before I could get my pants up, he grabbed my arm, pulled me down over his lap with my ass in the air, and squirted the bottle. I closed my eyes, gritted my teeth, waiting for the burn to start, but in two seconds, my pain was gone. Completely gone. I stood up and looked at Arick. He got up, patted me on the head, told me to pull my pants up, and walked out of the room. And we have never spoken of this incident since.

*HEATHER REESE is the author of the blog My Husband Ate All My Ice Cream. She's currently pushing out her fifth baby in her home in Central Iowa. She has a problem with over-sharing, and she cusses a lot. She'd also like to publicly apologize for naming her blog during a pregnancy-induced hormonal fit, after one lapse in judgment by her normally amazing husband.*

# Getting Lucky in Atlanta
## By Robyn Welling
### *Hollow Tree Ventures*

When my husband proposed, the first thing we did (besides make out) was start saving for our honeymoon. We didn't have a lot of money, but we knew that kids, mortgages, and reality in general would probably preclude another vacation alone together until after retirement—so with a long and wonderful lifetime stretching out before us, most of which would likely be spent at home on the couch cuddled up with the remote, we wanted to make the most of this opportunity.

We scraped enough pennies together for an amazing week in Key West, and frankly I was impressed that we only got locked out of our rental once. I knew I'd married well when, with only a small boost from me, my groom scaled the side of the building and hurled himself through an unlocked window, risking a trip to the ER but saving us from an expensive three A.M. pre-dawn call to either the property owner or a locksmith, whoever happened to be less inebriated at the time (Key West is fun like that). Yay, teamwork! That would've been embarrassing and inconvenient, but more importantly we didn't have any room in our squeaky-tight budget for pricey mistakes. *Whew!*

Getting home, we almost weren't so lucky.

To make it back to the airport from the southernmost tip of the country, we skipped across islands on bridges about two nanometers from being swallowed into the ocean, into downtown Miami, through the car rental kiosk, across the airport, and past security. With a bit of speeding, a moderate amount of jogging, and only one mild panic attack, we made it onto our flight—just in the nick of time!

And then we waited.

And waited.

*And waited.*

Excessive Floridian sunshine, or the airplane's engine falling out onto the tarmac, or *something* had caused a lengthy delay, but after liftoff we were able to shake the stress that built up during the first leg of our journey... only to start stressing about making our connecting flight in Atlanta.

We weren't *really* worried, though. After all, our connecting flight was with the same carrier. If these people could fling a chunk of people-stuffed aluminum across the country at five hundred miles per hour, I assumed they could figure out some way to tell *their own pilot* to wait up a minute until we got there.

We landed at nine at night with a generous forty-five second layover, so (just in case the pilot's walkie-talkie was broken, or the tardy airplane communicated with ground control via carrier pigeons that were released from the cockpit and sucked directly into the turbine) we wasted no time. We tore across the terminal, crisscrossed concourses. We glide-sprinted through congested conveyor belt walkways and resisted the urge to stop at Starbucks. Finally, our gate was in sight—and the plane was still there! Through our bleary-eyed travel exhaustion, we saw its silvery hull glinting with the promise of home.

But when we got closer, we noticed a group of people gathered around the boarding desk; a group that appeared to be one pitchfork shy of becoming an angry mob. The airline employees were sweating nervously in their red polyester vests.

"I'm sorry, but we're no longer boarding this flight," one Red Vest was saying as she loosened her matching neckerchief.

"But the plane is right there. *Right. There.*" Would-be passengers punctuated their frustration by desperately gesturing toward the idling aircraft.

"Yes, but once the doors are closed they can't be reopened."

Apparently, the ground crew's training didn't include basic information about how doors operate.

"But it's not our fault we missed boarding—*your plane* got us here late!" people were yelling. Red Vests One and Two had quickly become personally responsible for the entire airline's flight delays. Unreasonable? Maybe, but the increasingly outraged voice in my head had to side with the mob on this one.

"Please step over to the customer service desk if you'd like to reschedule your flight," she continued, as if there were some chance that we *didn't* want to reschedule. Maybe, having missed our flight, we'd just decide to unpack and spend the rest of our lives right there in Atlanta International's Concourse B.

At that moment I realized the futility of the situation—that no matter how tired and frustrated we were, we simply weren't getting home on that plane. None of us were. I felt deflated. My usually deep well of patience was suddenly as empty as the airport's sushi bar.

In contrast, an almost imperceptible change in the barometric pressure indicated that my husband was transitioning into Full-On Raging Temper Mode. He started to muscle toward the front of the mob, but I grabbed his arm. "Honey," I reasoned, "if they aren't letting Elderly Wheelchair Guy or Eight-Months Pregnant Lady onto the plane, they certainly aren't going to let us slip by. However," I said, my humanity having been stripped away by fatigue and injustice, "if we hurry up while they're all arguing, we can totally get in line ahead of them."

What else can you do? Off to customer service we shuffled, defeated and helpless, where we waited.

And waited.

*And waited.*

Half an airplane load of irate, stranded travelers used this time to vent loudly about the likelihood they were ever going to fly with this carrier again (zero percent, for the record). People were fuming about certain folks getting "special treatment" (hey, maybe *you* want to go to hell, Tank Top Dude, but I came to my senses and let Elderly Wheelchair Guy and Eight-Months Pregnant Lady cut in line). Things got even more heated when rumors drifted around that the airline wasn't exactly being cooperative.

I braced myself for the worst.

When we arrived at the counter, the customer service rep managed a terse but polite, "I'm Marcy, how can I help you?" instead of leaping into the path of an airport golf cart. I admired that.

My husband must've felt the same way because he didn't instantly explode, even though the vein in his forehead was still throbbing with a dangerous mixture of rage and stress hormones. "Marcy, you're a saint to deal with this," he sighed. "We seem to be stuck here. Can you get us home?"

"Certainly, sir." She took our information, tapped on her keyboard and offered, "I can get you on the next flight. It leaves at six tomorrow morning."

"TOMORROW?" we said in unison.

"Yes, that's the soonest flight. Would you like a list of local hotels and restaurants?"

"Doesn't the airline decide where they're putting us up?"

"Unfortunately, sir, since the delay was weather-related and not the fault of the airline, we're unable to comp passengers for overnight accommodations or meals," came her canned response.

While this information sank in, a fresh batch of testosterone surged into my husband's circulatory system and made its way toward his vocal cords. I, however, responded differently.

I burst into tears.

I sobbed, uncontrollably, alarming nearby strangers who surely thought I was a deranged person off her meds. "GREAT, now my wife is crying," my husband roared. At the end of his rope, he demanded to see a manager.

I put a hand on his arm and turned to Marcy, leaning in for some conspiratorial girl talk. Still stuttering through tears, I explained that we were on our honeymoon. We couldn't afford another night in a hotel or taxi fare or restaurant food, we didn't have any clean clothes in our carry-on bags, and suddenly I missed the kids so much my whole body ached.

Marcy's face softened. When she turned away for a moment I stole a peek at my husband, who was no longer irate. If he'd been surprised by my outburst, he was over it. Instead, he nodded encouragement and winked. I winked back. Without a word, we both realized my insane spectacle of venting was having an unintentional side effect: *actual sympathy*.

One week in, and our marriage was already working like a well-oiled machine, chugging toward a common goal—my pitiful weeping softened his gruff demands, his assertiveness gave purpose to my tearful over-sharing of all our personal information. Finally, Marcy glanced side-eyed down the counter at the rows of other passengers and customer service reps. "Look, there's nothing I can do, but go over to those courtesy phones. Talk to the manager. It's out of my hands," she said a little more loudly, "but maybe they can help you." Then softly, "I'll close my window until you get back so you don't have to wait in line again."

I resisted the urge to kiss Marcy on the mouth, and my husband and I trudged off to the courtesy phones, where I retold the whole story to the manager, still whimpering pathetically. When he put me on hold, I wiped my cheeks and grinned.

"Are you faking this? Because if you are, it's pure genius."

"No, I'm a hot mess—but it seems to be working, doesn't it?" We hid in the courtesy phone booth and giggled like scheming teenagers, high on exhaustion and airport overdose.

The manager came back on the line and instructed us to return to the desk. Marcy was waiting with vouchers for breakfast and dinner, and a free one-night stay in a posh hotel. She gave us overnight kits with clean T-shirts and toiletries. No matter how many times we thanked her (quietly, to avoid backlash from people who hadn't had the sense to come completely unhinged and were therefore forced to sleep on the airport floor outside Cinnabon), she insisted she had nothing to do with it. I had my doubts.

"Girl, you're just lucky you caught me at my lady time." *Oh Marcy, as if I didn't love you already.*

My husband and I, still broke and weary but satisfied, dragged ourselves to the hotel shuttle. "That was awesome," he said, squeezing my hand. "If I weren't already sure I'd married the right woman, I am now."

"We certainly do make a good team," I replied, squeezing back.

To this day, we still don't have a lot of money. But ever since that very first week, we've known we have something in our marriage that's far more valuable than any amount of cash: teamwork. Not to mention, we have something even *more* valuable than that: the ability to use teamwork to get stuff we can't afford because we don't have any money.


*ROBYN WELLING is a freelance writer and humorist at <u>Hollow Tree Ventures</u>, where she isn't afraid to embarrass herself—and frequently does. She also writes for awesome sites like <u>In The Powder Room</u> (where she's also the Editorial Assistant), <u>NickMom</u>, CraftFail, and* The Huffington Post. *She's been named a Must-Follow Humor Blog by BlogHer and co-authored two best-selling humor anthologies,* I Just Want To Pee Alone *and "*You Have Lipstick On Your Teeth,*" yet her kids still don't think she's funny. Her goals include becoming independently wealthy, followed by world domination and getting her children to clean their rooms. Until then, she'll just fold laundry and write about the shortcuts she takes on her journey to becoming a somewhat passable wife, mother, and human being; if history is any guide, she'll miss the mark entirely. You can find her avoiding responsibility on <u>Facebook</u>, <u>Twitter</u>, and <u>Pinterest</u>.*

# Rehearsal Dinner Roofie
## By Lori Wescott
### *Loripalooza*

It was a lovely outdoor garden affair and the food was delicious. All our loved ones were there for our rehearsal dinner on that May evening in 2003. I sat at a table with my fiancé along with his two brothers who were to serve as his groomsmen, and my two sisters who were my bridesmaids.

The rehearsal had gone well and I was finally breathing a sigh of relief that things were going to come together perfectly the next day. My southern Baptist parents were mingling well with my future in-laws, of which I was gaining two sets.

After dessert was served my husband-to-be arose from the table and decided to say a few words. This was somewhat of a surprise to me because he didn't like public speaking. I had butterflies in my stomach, but sitting there watching the man I loved charismatically addressing our new families made me love him even more.

"First of all, I want to thank all of you for being a part of this very special occasion," he started. "Lori and I are so grateful for your love and support. I know some of you traveled very far to be here and that means a lot to us."

He walked over and placed his hand on his Grandmother's shoulder. It had been several years since her stroke and while she re-mained alert and mobile, she had never regained the ability to speak. She and her late husband had shared a bond with my fiancé that was very special. We all teared up as he spoke to her about how thankful he was for the influence she and his Grandfather had been on him.

My younger sister whispered to me, "Lori, this is so sweet." As I smiled at her I couldn't help thinking about how lucky I was to be marrying the man of my dreams. The next day I would be Mrs. Brantley Wescott.

Brantley's speech then strayed from reminiscing about his child-hood and a smile came across his face as he began his next story. "Some of you may not have heard about how Lori and I met and it's actually a pretty interesting story," he began.

The butterflies in my stomach were replaced with heart palpitations. There was a split-second triangle of eye contact between my sisters and I. They would be in charge of damage control if the situation warranted it. *This precaution would surely not be necessary, but it never hurts to have a plan-B*, I thought.

My handsome fiancé continued, "Most of you know that we met at work, but you may not have known that Lori asked *me* out on our first date *and* made the first move."

I remained calm although I could hear my sisters whispering. They were arguing over how to create a distraction if this dissertation of his got any worse. Apparently, neither one of them wanted to fake choking and be given the Heimlich maneuver by the other. I took several sips of wine and tried not to notice my Dad staring at his plate and my Mom chugging her ice water like a good southern Baptist while wishing it was wine.

The speech continued, "You probably didn't know this either, but the first conversation I ever had with her parents was over the phone from a hospital when I had to call them at five o'clock in the morning and tell them she was about to have an emergency appendectomy. Now, keep in mind that this was only a couple of days after our first date and there I was having to basically tell her Mom and Dad that while staying overnight at my apartment she had gotten sick."

As if that weren't enough he then walked over to my Dad, gave him a gentle punch to the shoulder and said, "She wasn't as pristine as you thought she was after all."

I looked over at my damage control team to see them main-lining Sauvignon Blanc. The damage had been done and my eyes glazed over as I tried to slip into a fugue state.

What the hell was he thinking? True, he had not been the one to actually break my beaver dam, but that was a far cry from being the loose hussy I had just been painted to look like.

One of my sisters stood and interrupted the sea of nervous laughter by shouting, "Who wants more pie?" while the other one gently tackled Brantley and sat him back down in his chair. With a forkful of something suddenly shoved into his mouth he was unable to continue what he thought was a hilarious and heart-warming story of how we met and fell in love.

With the great orator and husband-to-be seated back at my side I managed a smile as I whispered in his ear, "What the fuck is wrong with you? We are so lucky your Grandmother can't talk because I don't think we would like what she has to say."

It was as if he hadn't heard a word I said. "Was I funny?" he asked. "Because I took some of that Klonipin the doctor gave me to help with anxiety before I presented my doctoral thesis. God, I hate public speaking. I don't even remember what I said just now. I felt kind of floaty, but I think it went pretty well. Are you crying because you're happy, or stressed out about the wedding? Because this Klonipin really, really helps."

It has been ten years since our loved ones' ears were forever stained with that speech. Miraculously, we're still married. Less miraculously, I'm still trying to prove I'm not a whore and Klonipin still really, really helps.

*LORI WESCOTT is a trophy wife and humorist residing in Nashville, TN. Her blog, Loripalooza has been making people laugh since 2008 and is the home of Awkward Smoking Pictures. Her main goals in life have long since been accomplished, so now she is trying to avoid drugs and taking time to focus on her mission to stop duck face photography with a campaign called "Moms Against Sexy Faces" (MASF). She co-authored, "You Have Lipstick On Your Teeth" in 2013 and Chicken Soup For The Soul: Family Matters in 2010. When Lori isn't blogging you can find her on Twitter or at her kitchen table making really terrible crafts with her son. She also enjoys spending time with wine and taking very short walks on the beach.*

# The Five Stages of ~~Grief~~ Dating and Marriage
## By Leanne Shirtliffe
### *Ironic Mom*

It is a truth universally acknowledged that I wanted to marry Mr. Darcy. However, since Jane Austen's hero is fictional and since the other Mr. Darcy (a.k.a. Colin Firth) has been happily married to an Italian hottie since—well—forever, I had to settle for my husband, a guy named Chris.

My life with Chris has been more *Bridget Jones Diary* than *Pride and Prejudice*, more fluorescent diner than candlelight dinner, more Canada than Cannes.

To this day, some sixteen years since we started dating, we seem to invite minor catastrophes into our relationship. And I'm not even talking about our twins, who are now tweens.

In fact, my relationship with Chris kind of mirrors Kubler-Ross's stages of grief, except that no one has died. Yet.

Here, then, are my five stages of ~~grief~~ dating and marriage:

**STAGE ONE: Denial (or, "Are You Freaking Kidding Me?")**

In the beginning, there was denial in the desert. Chris and I met in Bahrain, a tiny island country in the middle of the Persian Gulf where I was frequently mistaken for an Eastern European hooker. I'd fled Canada and a failed engagement and opted to teach overseas. I wasn't looking for love; I was looking for adventure. I got both.

At first, I denied this relationship was going anywhere. On our first movie date, we were just two foreigners sitting side-by-side in a highly air-conditioned theater filled with hundreds of Bahrainis watching Leo and Kate kiss, or what we assumed was kissing since local authorities blacked out the touchy-touchy parts.

Less than halfway through James Cameron's epic, our faces turned blue, illuminated by the Indiglo of my digital watch. That beacon flashed throughout the theater, periodically announcing that I despised the movie.

We started whispering.

"Thank God it sinks quickly."

"I have underwear that is older than Leo."

"If the whole movie is a flashback, how can Rose remember scenes that she wasn't even in?"

"*My Heart Will Go On*? Like this freaking movie."

"What are the lyrics: *'Near... far'*? Is Celine Dion covering Grover's *Sesame Street* segment on opposites?"

There was no denying it. The first date's score: Snark 1, Relationship 1, Movie 0.

## STAGE TWO: Anger (or, Lizards, Hair Dryers, and Engagements)

What would the logical reaction when you *know* your boyfriend is going to propose to you on a specific date?

Anger.

It's not used in many engagement ring ads, but anger can make Tiffany blue seem just a bit brighter.

Chris and I were in one of our falling-apart cars driving out to the Bahraini desert. It was Friday, the Muslim holy day, which meant the highway was empty, and people—including my students—were praying for me.

Two weeks before, Chris had booked the date and told me we were going for a picnic to our favorite spot in the desert...in the heat of the summer. Then we were going out for a fancy dinner.

"That seems kind of stupid," I said. "What do I wear? Hiking gear or a dress?"

"Just wear hiking gear," Chris said. "It's good enough."

*Good enough.* We aimed high in our relationship.

Out of the city, a massive pipeline skirted the quiet highway and Chris's quieter car. Heat rose in waves off the sand dunes.

Then, an outburst. "Sonofa – "

"What's wrong?" I asked.

Chris pointed to the heat gauge. "Look how high it is."

I leaned over. Yikes. We had no cell phones, we were out in the abandoned desert on the holy day, and it was 114 degrees.

"I'm turning on the heater," Chris said. "It'll draw some heat away from the motor."

He continued driving, heat blasting through the vents and the windows. Had Thelma and Louise experienced this, they wouldn't have waited until the end of the movie to drive their car off a cliff.

I suggested, "We could turn arou—"

"No! We're. Going. On. A. Picnic."

The heat gauge crept down and, like our tempers, moved from boiling to simmer. The drive continued in sweltering silence.

Then again. Louder this time. "Mother – "

Brakes squealed. I saw a giant lizard—called a dhub—skitter across the highway, under the car.

*If we kill a lizard, is it a sign from God, from Allah, from the freaking universe that we shouldn't get married?*

In a Linda Blair head spin, I glared out the rear window as the car skidded, leaving a trail of rubber.

The three-foot lizard kept running, out from under the car, into the sand dunes.

"You almost killed that," I said.

Chris grimaced. "Not even close."

We arrived at our desert spot, the same place he'd taken me on our third date nearly two years ago when the romance was fresh, like sheets hung on the line. This time, I felt sweat drip down my armpits, which is pretty much how every romantic engagement story starts.

"How about we leave the picnic stuff in the car and just hike up?" he said.

We climbed our mini mountain. The wind blew hard, like a giant industrial hair dryer stuck on high. By the time we hiked to our picnic destination, we felt like two donuts fresh out of the deep fryer that had been covered in powdered sugar.

The sun reflected hard off the sand, and I shielded my eyes. I looked east and saw the Persian Gulf. I looked west and saw the Persian Gulf.

"Coast-to-coast," Chris said.

I nodded.

He stepped closer to me. Our sweat intermingled for a moment. "Marry me, OK?

"Are you actually serious?"

He nodded.

"OK," I said. "Can we leave now?"

"Sure. We should get going. In case we don't make it."

We'd been engaged for two minutes and were already talking about not making it.

**STAGE THREE: Bargaining (or, Grandma, Linoleum, and Bacon)**

Chris' grandma was legendary. Family lore claimed she had a direct line to God and that she jogged on the spot twenty minutes a day while saying the rosary. I haven't had that much success multi-tasking since I studied for college finals while simultaneously eating Kraft Dinner and shouting out wrong Jeopardy answers.

In her snug apartment, we ate a dinner of pork chops doused in Campbell's mushroom soup and freezer-burnt ice cream at four thirty in the afternoon. Teeth were optional.

Grandma helped us pull out the hideaway bed in the couch. "Leanne will sleep here," she instructed.

She placed a blanket on the floor of the kitchen at the base of the avocado-colored fridge. "Chris will sleep here."

We hugged Grandma, who retired to her bedroom six feet away. "I'll pray for you both," she said.

Chris would need those prayers as he slept on the linoleum with the fridge clicking and buzzing every twenty minutes throughout the long night.

Morning meant church, even though it was Tuesday, followed by a farmer's breakfast at the café.

More hugs goodbye and we left on our five-hour return trip.

We listened to music and watched grain elevators—the prairie's phallic symbol—grow from miles away and then shrink behind us.

After miles more of silence, we began talking at the same time.

We both stopped.

"You go first—" he said.

"No, you go first—"

"No, no, you start," Chris said.

I could tell that he was not going to give in on this bargain.

"I was just going to tell you about my dream." Nothing makes driving on the flattest road on earth more exciting than talking about your dreams.

"Go ahead," Chris insisted.

"OK," I said. "I had this dream. I was pregnant, very pregnant. And it was a good thing. It was good timing for us. And I woke up feeling all warm and fuzzy. Almost glowing, you know?"

"Oh," he said. "Wow, that's really nice, I guess."

The summer sun streamed through the window, and I smiled. My eyes looked out at the highway ahead of us, which remained blissfully lizard-less. My big breakfast warmed my stomach.

"Oh, hey," I said. "What were you going to say?"

"It doesn't matter."

"Yes, yes, it does."

"No, I'll tell you some other time."

"No," I said. "I want to know what you were going to say when I started talking."

"Well, I'm glad you went first," he said, pausing to scan the horizon, "because I was just going to say that bacon makes my lips chapped."

## STAGE FOUR: Depression (or, My Husband's Midlife Minivan Crisis)

Somehow, we popped out two kids at once, both of whom list bacon as one of their top-five foods. We drove a minivan, not so affectionately nicknamed "The Loser Cruiser."

Just when I thought our lives couldn't become more suburban, I drove home to a scene I was unprepared for. I careened my commuter car onto our street and saw it: our minivan had grown giant white and blue flames on the side and across the hood.

"What did you do?" I asked, as I bounded in through the front door.

Chris started laughing. "I pimped the minivan."

"You certainly did."

"Are the flames permanent?" I asked.

He answered my question with a question. "Do you know I had to order them from another country? I got to choose the shapes of the flames and the colors."

I breathed. Kind of.

Chris continued. "Hey, it was cheaper than a subwoofer. Plus, don't you think it's hilarious?"

"You were going for some sort of suburban irony?"

He grinned. "Yup."

"I don't think people are going to get the irony. They're going to see a loser who thinks his minivan is cool."

"Then they're stupid," he said.

"People tend to be literal, you know."

"So you don't like them?" He didn't wait for an answer. "The flames almost cover up where the kids carved their names on the sliding doors."

"Almost?"

"And hey, you won't lose the van in the parking lot anymore."

"True. And I won't have to lock it either."

**STAGE FIVE: Acceptance (or, Sound Bytes from the Flea Market)**

Because flipping dead people's crap is Chris' hobby, every weekend he sets up at a local flea market, located at the corner of scuzzy and trendy. I've had no choice but to catapult to acceptance, with occasional detours back to anger and bargaining. "This is something I'm going to do until I die," Chris says. If it gets the suburban detritus out of our garage, then it's worth the sacrifice.

Being a vendor at a local flea market is comic gold. In the past year, Chris has started sentences with all of the following:

"So, you know the guy at the flea market who thinks I ordered you from Russia?"

"So, there's the balding guy who walks around with shoe polish on his head..."

"So, this guy wearing flip flops and a bathrobe comes up to my table..."

"So, this woman—she's a vendor—she wears ski goggles for the whole day..."

"So, this guy in his sixties who never removes his combat helmet..."

Really, what choice is there but to accept that this is the cycle of marriage?

This man, who does a sperm-whale puppet show for our kids at a restaurant...

This man, who when I tell him "I love you," looks up from his book and says, "Sorry? I didn't hear you. I was reading about executions during the Soviet terror-famine."

This man, who describes what it must be like for me to be married to him: "It's like being drunk. There is some euphoria followed by a lot of down periods."

This man, who indulges me as I re-watch the DVD of Mr. Darcy diving into the pond at Pemberley for the umpteenth time.

This husband of mine, who smiles when I say, "Can you just sit there, rub my neck, and not say anything stupid?"

And he shuts up.

Good grief, that's acceptance.


*LEANNE SHIRTLIFFE is a humor writer, a mom to nine-year-old twins, and the author of two parenting books,* DON'T LICK THE MINIVAN: And Other Things I Never Thought I'd Say to My Kids *(2013) and* MOMMYFESTO: We Swear...Because We Have Kids *(November 2014). Her first picture book,* THE CHANGE YOUR NAME STORE, *will be published in May (2014). Leanne is the woman behind* Ironic Mom, *where the motto is"If you can't laugh at yourself, laugh at your kids"; it was named to Babble's Top 100 list in 2013. Leanne writes for Nickelodeon's NickMom.com, blogs for* The Huffington Post, *and co-runs StuffKidsWrite.com ("Like Stuff Adults Write. But Funnier."). She's been published by the* Globe and Mail, *the* Christian Science Monitor, *and the* Calgary Herald. *Leanne once won the caber toss championship in Bahrain and chased transvestites in Bangkok. She and her family live in Canada because they like complaining about the weather.*

# Cleanup In Aisle Four
## By Suzanne Fleet
### *Toulouse and Tonic*

Near the end of the long, winding road of my dating days, I found myself in a conundrum. Despite my vows to the contrary, I was in a relationship with a man who was much younger, a bit thinner – *and* shorter than me, should I have on even a kitten heel. Not only had I broken a sacred vow by dating a man whose ass was smaller than mine – indignity of indignities, he even had prettier hair than I did.

So pretty, in fact, that I spent languid hours running my fingers through it as we talked, alternating between admiration and jealousy.

Like a lion, Gabe was proud of his hair too. When he was on-stage with his band, his shoulder-length locks put on a show of their own behind the drum-kit. Now falling forward into his eyes, lazily becoming a curtain for his face as the beat slows into sleepiness. Now bouncing rhythmically side-to-side while he keeps the beat. Now voraciously slung back and vibrantly air-born as the music crescendos.

And too, he used it for flirting. Looking down and letting the tendrils sway in front of his face like rope swings, glancing back up in my direction, biting his lip, smiling a small smile and then "shyly" looking away – a move I later learned he'd practiced a thousand times in the mirror.

As I gave in to the relationship after months of digging my heels in the pearly Destin, Florida sand, I began to discover that this band boy wasn't what I'd expected. He was smart, he was kind, he was loyal and playful … and he was an epic metrosexual.

It turned out Gabe liked being at my house when he was off the road for more than just the pleasure of my company. Almost as tempting for him was the bounty of expensive hair care products like Bumble & Bumble, Aveda, and L'Occitane lining every contour of my shower.

After we'd been together long enough to stop fighting every time we drank too much but not too long to make occasional decisions out of passion, he spent a few lazy days at my house while the band was off the road.

## I Just Want to Be Alone

I woke one morning to find him leaning into the bathroom mirror, chin to chest, eyes trained upward on the inch of dark hair at his roots.

"This looks terrible," he says dejectedly. "I need my highlights touched up but I'm dead broke."

I brighten up. "I can totally do that for you! All we need is a box of color from the drugstore!"

"Ooooooh, I don't know about that." Gabe recoils a bit, protectively tucking his hair behind one ear and turning away from me as if I might hit him.

"It'll be easy!" I sell it with my eagerness and grossly unfounded self-confidence. "Come on, you'll look great!" I make a dismissive swish through the air with my hand. "I color my hair all the time."

There was *some* exaggeration in the statement as I had only performed the most minor of touch-ups to my roots a couple of times.

"Really?" Gabe squeaks, his face schizophrenic as hope and doubt fight for control of the same features.

"You'll look hot!" I say, looping my purse over my arm. "Let's go pick out a color."

We make the two-minute drive to Walgreen's and hold hands as we stroll the aisle dedicated to hair. There are so many shades of blond that Gabe starts to get into the spirit. Champagne, chamomile, butternut, macadamia ... the subtle differences entrance us as we hold the boxes together comparing the models' shiny strands.

We settle on the *Extreme Blond* highlighting kit – the hair-color equivalent of strapping on a snowboard for the first time and catching the lift straight to a black diamond run.

While I'm not unaware that working with bleach is considered tricky, even by professionals, I'm quickly comforted by the box, which assures us it's both "nice" and "easy."

Gabe becomes quiet on the drive home, turning the box over and over in his hands like a talisman that might bring him luck.

In the driveway, I turn the car off but he makes no move to get out. His bowed head begs for a moment of silence that I'm unable to grant him.

"Come on, stop worrying! How hard can it be?"

After he showers, I place him in a chair and drape a fluffy white towel over his shoulders, then bend over, giving him a warm, reassuring squeeze. He flashes me a crooked smile and I skip about the house gathering all the necessary tools: comb, hair clips, color, paintbrush, cocktail ...

Half an hour in, it's proving to be a whole box of fun. In my left hand, I hold a lightly sweating margarita glass, partially melted ice cubes clinking percussively as I move – in my right, a small paintbrush with which I enthusiastically dab faintly chemical-smelling goo onto Gabe's beautiful canvas of hair. Maroon 5's "Songs About Jane" plays in the background.

I paint. I stand back and consider my work. *Hmmm*, I think, tilting my head to one side and regarding my masterpiece. I add more bleach here and there in flourishes that can best be described as the abstract impressionism style of art.

We're chatting and laughing and I'm painting and tippling, and Gabe only wonders aloud a few times if I should possibly consider using some foils to keep the bleach from touching the rest of his hair.

"Naaah," I say, draining my glass. "Totally unnecessary. But you know what is necessary? Another drink."

After marginally following the box's instructions, I lead Gabe to the kitchen sink. He places his head in the basin and I scrub the bleach out. Gently towel-drying his hair, I rise up on my tiptoes for a look at my handy-work. *Ummm, that looks a little funny*, I think. But I've had my hair colored enough to know that it doesn't show up properly until it's dry.

Gabe tilts his face towards me and I give him the kiss of the damned.

He heads for the bathroom and I follow – a fizzy bubble of uneasiness vibrating up my windpipe.

"I can't wait to see it." He looks at me over his shoulder, his face bright with hope. I offer him a clown's smile, then loiter skittishly in the door frame as he begins to dry his hair.

Soon, all the spectacular colors of fall in the North Carolina mountains begin to reveal themselves in wide splotches across his crown. I see no blond, subtle or extreme, but instead a veritable buffet of orange and brown in shades previously only known to the ugliest of calico cats.

The drier his hair gets, the more strain shows on his face. He's still holding the dryer on his hair but his eyes have become watery, his open mouth emitting a kind of stutter-laugh/wail combination.

I haven't moved from the doorway, but I shift my weight back and forth from leg to leg, caught in a strange emotional vortex, bastard siblings of inappropriate giggling and quite appropriate crying trying to elbow their way out of my larynx first.

Gabe turns the dryer off and all is silent. He looks into the mirror, shoulders slumped. Without warning, he makes a high-pitched sound like that of a copulating cat. He looks at his reflection some more. Makes the sound again.

I melt away to the bedroom, chewing on a fingernail, wondering if I've wrecked things with my slurry overconfidence. I slink out periodically, peering around corners measuring his mood, and finally perch lightly next to him on the sofa, both of us staring straight ahead into murky waters.

I put my head on his shoulder tentatively, my hair catching on the beanie he's now wearing.

A deep sigh. "I'm sorry. I really thought I could do it."

An answering sigh. "I know you did."

Gabe shakes his head, then glances at me with a lopsided grin. "Look at it this way. While not funny now, it'll make a great story to tell our kids and grandkids someday."

We snuggle in, sitting there in the kind of silence that comes after you've said just exactly enough to know that what you have can survive not only a cleanup in aisle four but so very much more.

*SUZANNE FLEET is the writer behind the award-winning blog, <u>Toulouse & Tonic</u>, and mom to two stinky boys, who together with her good-natured husband, give her shitloads of funny writing material. Suzanne is one of Circle of Moms Top 25 Funny Moms, a* Huffington Post *contributor and a proud co-author of the best-selling books,* I Just Want To Pee Alone *and* "You Have Lipstick on Your Teeth." *Keep the laughs coming by following her on <u>Facebook</u>, <u>Twitter</u>, and <u>Pinterest</u>.*

# He Knocks Me Up and Stinks Me Out
## By Stephanie Jankowski
### *When Crazy Meets Exhaustion*

My husband is a *doer*, which is to say he is a pain in my whole ass.

I know how fortunate I am to have a man whose butt cheeks are not permanently imprinted into the cushions of our couch. He is a go-getter. A hustler. An ambitious SOB who grabs life by the balls and gets shit done.

It's just that he has the world's *worst* timing.

Take, for instance, the fancy-schmancy wedding we were invited to attend a few summers ago. Like, so fancy that my bedazzled flip-flops were deemed unacceptable footwear.

As I rushed to apply my make-up, reminding myself to swipe mascara across *both* eyes, I noticed the clock nagging me for running late (again). Why was it that I struggled to get anywhere on time? Oh, yeah: **kids**.

*Turn off the TV!*

*Refill sippy cups!*

*Change a diaper!*

*Hurry! Hurry! HURRY!!*

A final glance in the mirror to confirm the inevitable: mascara on only one eye. Sonofa …

*Curl the hair!*

*Pull on the Spanx!*

*Sign the card!*

*Hurry! Hurry! HURRY!!*

And where was my husband in the midst of the madness? Out-side staining the deck, *of course*.

It bears mentioning that the man was unsuccessful in washing the dark brown stain from his hands and arms, so when we finally arrived at the church just in time to race the bride and her father down the aisle, it was with speckled hands that resembled liver spots o' poo with which my husband congratulated the new couple. Black-ened fingernails, stray shrapnel on his cheek, a faint odor of lumber.

We like to keep it classy.

Physically incapable of prioritizing a to-do list, my husband continually initiates ill-timed and irrelevant undertakings. Gross hands at a black tie event is one thing; almost poisoning me while pregnant is another.

The year was 2009 and I was *this close* to popping with our first born. As any man preparing for the birth of his first child, my husband found it necessary to maintain our landscaping to the degree of insanity.

*Naturally*.

I don't know if it was a father's instinct or the male version of nesting, but I have yet to find another of his species match the obsessive affinity for edging and aerating that he displayed that summer. It was ridiculous. Loads of mulch delivered, grass seed planted, and I don't know which he was more excited about: the free rocks he snagged from a nearby landslide or the impending arrival of our baby.

Probably the rocks.

Meanwhile, I concerned myself with more pressing matters, like the imminent reality that a small child's head would soon destroy my pelvic floor in a nearby hospital. As I washed adorable onesies in Dreft and kept diligent notes in my baby journal, my husband was preoccupied with thoughts of gasoline.

*Gasoline*.

For the lawn mower. For the weed whacker. You know, all of the necessary equipment with which to welcome a newborn.

MUST. HAVE. MORE. GASOLINE.

He tossed the "empty" gas can in the back of our SUV and took off for a refill. When he returned, the stench was undeniable.

**Me:** What the hell?

**Him:** Yeah, that can wasn't empty after all. A little gas spilled.

*A little* being the understatement of the year. The SUV carpet was soaked through and the nauseating odor was the kind that accosted both nostrils and brain cells.

**Him:** Don't worry; we'll leave the windows down and it'll air out in a few days.

As we drove to the hospital *the very next day* with me laboring in the back seat, I felt each pang of my ripening cervix only a little more than the twinges of fury that boiled within as I breathed in noxious fumes and screamed obscenities about our baby being born cross-eyed because my husband just had to have his *motherfucking gasoline.*

I will say this: as we pulled away from our house, with my back breaking in two, sweat pooling in all of my lady crevices courtesy of the sweltering July heat, I noted that our lawn was the nicest on the block.

Odds are that a man would only knock up and stink out his wife once during their marriage, but my Probability and Statistics teacher of a husband lives to defy the odds.

Less than two years after the Gasoline Debacle of 2009, I lay on our couch a beached whale mere days away from delivering our daughter. Unfolded infant clothes heaped in laundry baskets, the baby journal incomplete, I struggled to find a comfortable position that didn't put my hips to sleep underneath the sheer weight of *myself.* And, right on time, my husband returned to his lunacy.

What was on his We're-Having-Another-Baby-To-Do List?

Pack hospital bag? HA!

Ensure proper installation of car seat? Pffft.

Rub wife's cankles? *Riiiiiight.*

Mr. Most Inefficient Manager of Time EVER decided that our oven needed cleaning. With his swollen wife attempting a nap in the adjoining room, and his toddler son snoozing upstairs, my helpful husband set the self-clean option for the very first time and walked away.

A few minutes later, I started smelling … something. I chalked it up to my hypersensitive pregnant nose, and tried again to wrangle my gorging belly around some pillows to rest.

Then, the coughing. The watering eyes. The gagging.

Minutes later, I was engrossed in a haze of toxic gases, choking as I rushed to open windows, or at least heave myself out the front door onto the painstakingly manicured lawn as to escape the putrid cloud

that had enveloped the first floor of my home. But it was too late.
A scent reminiscent of decaying flesh assaulted the air, the drapes,
my hair and clothing. And oh, my fetus.

When darling husband returned and inquired as to why I was in
a sleeping bag on the front stoop, I hurled the oven's instruction
manual at him, pointing to some helpful information I had highlight-
ed for his perusal:

**WARNING**: *Users of this appliance are hereby warned that when the oven
is engaged in the self-clean cycle, especially in its initial use, there may be
some low-level exposure to...carbon monoxide (and other) substances
known...to cause cancer or reproductive harm.*

**Him:** Huh. I didn't see that part.
**Me:** Clearly.
**Him:** You're mad?
**Me:** Affirmative. You're going to want to keep your distance.
**Him:** Should I bring you chocolate?
**Me:** Should you even have to ask?

As I write this essay, I am seven months pregnant with our third
child, eagerly awaiting the new and exciting ways my husband will
almost kill me. We have already compared our We're-Having-AN-
OTHER-Baby-To-Do-Lists and they look something like this:

**Me:**
Wash baby's clothes in whatever detergent is avail
able
Find baby journal
Buy diapers
Lather stretch marks in cocoa butter
Kegels, Kegels, Kegels
**Him:**
Paint basement steps (so my wife will slip and fall
to her demise)
Install crown molding (the dust will suffocate my
loved ones)

## I Just Want to Be Alone

Make and freeze mass quantities of kielbasa and
'kraut (as to promote explosive diarrhea)
Because nothing says *welcome to the world, new baby!* like a fog of
residual sauerkraut farts.


*STEPHANIE JANKOWSKI loves words, hates math, and has a penchant for making people uncomfortable with honesty. An English teacher by trade and a smack-talker by nature, her blog, <u>When Crazy Meets Exhaustion</u>, affords an acceptable medium for her verbal diarrhea. Stephanie credits her parents for raising her with just enough dysfunction to make her funny, and thanks her exceptionally tolerant husband and their two (soon-to-be-three!) wonderful children for their love, support, and perpetual writing fodder. You should hang with her on <u>Facebook</u>, and <u>Twitter</u> because that's what a decent person would do.*

# Saint Spouse
## By Bethany Thies
### *Bad Parenting Moments*

It is said that no man is an island ... regardless of how many times he attempts to place his coconuts near your face. This must be true because where would I be if not for my man? Besides somewhere else. But would that somewhere else be as interesting? Or would it laugh as heartily at my jokes? Or would it reload the dishwasher because I didn't do it correctly the first time? I don't know. One shudders to imagine.

The thing about marriage is that it requires so much compromise. And, naturally, someone is going to come into the marriage being better at The Yield. In fact, I say a lengthy marriage requires it. Someone is always going to come in with horns down and nostrils flaring. That requires that the other person run away as quickly as possible while waving the white flag. Certainly not the red flag, because I don't want to be that poor woman who accidentally ran over her spouse sixty-five times. Someone is the bull. Someone must be the china shop. We all have important roles to play.

My husband has always been the most rational of the two of us. He loves me enough to acquiesce even when I'm wrong, which ... of course, has never happened. But let's just say in some fantasy world where feet are on faces and no one smells after using natural deodorant that this was true. Pretend I was wrong, if you can. He'd make sure I still felt the victor because, not unlike the Mafia, I know people. And the fact that all of these people are also separate personalities of mine makes me much more frightening than some criminal mastermind with a Tommy gun and a raging case of syphilis.

As the self appointed bull, please know what great strength of character it takes for me to say, in print, that my husband is a saint. I know this because he remains married to me no matter how many times I write about his penis, procedures done to his penis, or how little attention I actually pay to his penis, other than the deep attention I provide it during my creative writing process.

I also know this to be true because of all of the times our no longer mutual friends have said:

# I Just Want to Be Alone

"Your husband is a saint!"and,

"How did such a gallant saint of a man end up with you?" or,

"We all just love your husband so much!" or,

"You're a bitch."

It's hard to argue with the throngs of people who have already implicitly stated that they won't serve as my character witness at the trial.

The thing is my husband is indeed a saint, but he is also a husband, and in the ratio of sainthood versus normal annoying traits of earth-bound husbands he is also maddening and terribly un-saintly. Someone has to keep his saintliness in perspective.

While I'm fully aware that he deserves to be named after some formal, saintly establishment, perhaps a Wi-Fi enabled, multi-use conference room in heaven, I also recognize that he may get to heaven just that much sooner if he doesn't stop leaving his Maglite on the top of my decorative tin hutch. And, if you tell me he is a saint for allowing me a full hutch for my decorative tins, one of my more aggressive personalities may punch you repeatedly until you see things my way.

I would argue that simply being married to me isn't enough of a reason to be eligible for sainthood. You should save babies from ravenous dingoes or something psycho-sociologically relevant in order to be named a saint, but apparently having a shrewish humorist for a wife is close enough to inventing the vaccine that eradicated polio. So, congratulations, Honey *ironic, slow clap.*

I'm not bitter, per se, but I am maybe just the tiniest, teeny-tiny bit tired of hearing about how excellently excellent he is even if it's completely true. Because, let's face it, perfect people are annoying. So imagine how difficult it is to be married to someone so wonderful. I know, it's tough being me. Sympathy gifts of mid-range boxed Pinot Noir will be graciously accepted.

In fact, when I sat down to write this piece I thought, FINALLY I can really tell everyone how terrible it is being married to this perfect saint of a guy, and I just knew women everywhere would rally around me – clapping together their own temporarily-dis-placed-by-a-mag-light decorative tins in agreement and solidarity. It would be like the sound of a thousand, vaginally adorned bells ring-ing, and at last I would be vindicated from another day of righteous awesomeness from the world's greatest husband.

But when scouring my brain to freedom-write all of the things he does that annoy me, I realized that I am an unsympathetic character in my own marriage which is, to be fair, entirely his fault for being so likeable. What an asshole.

For example: can I really complain that my husband tells me that he'll never grant me a divorce because he loves me so much? Well, I shouldn't, but ... watch me try.

Or can I complain about the fact that he tells me I should get out more? Or that he fully supports my writing career even though using the word career to describe my career is a mockery to the word ca-reer? I shouldn't, but, oh, just try and stop me.

Here is my chance to shout from the rooftops about how dirty he leaves the bathroom and how he constantly tells me that my ass looks fat in my skinny jeans and how he wishes I gave blowjobs like that gold-hearted hooker from the Bay Area he once knew. But I can't, be-cause, sadly, none of that is true.

He's so incredibly selfish to give me absolutely nothing of sub-stance to complain about.

Honey, you win. You're a goddamned saint. Are you happy now?

Oh, don't you dare tell me that you're only happy if I am. Don't you dare!

Oh, my GOD, he said it. What does a gal have to do around here to get a lack of respect?

Sigh. I love you, honey. Quick, take the remote before I change my mind.

# I Just Want to Be Alone

*BETHANY THIES is a writer and the proud mother to four, young Vikings. She is the author of <u>Bad Parenting Moments</u> and the chronically unread poetry blog Room for Cream. She can often be found searching for her self respect, keys, discount non-perishables, and a bathroom lock her children cannot pick. Bethany is a staff writer for In the Powder Room, blogs for* The Huffington Post *and has had original works published in three best-selling anthologies. She contributes to her local, independent newspaper and can be heard on Vermont radio every month. Her children are unimpressed.*

# Saving the Knight
## By Kathy Glow
### *kissing the frog*

He wasn't exactly tall, dark, and handsome, but I learned pretty quickly he had the capacity to become a prince. Holding doors, cracking jokes, fawning over his twenty nieces and nephews, and eventually warming up showers so I could get in first, I knew he was a keeper pretty quickly.

He'll say he knew I was "the one" when I was talking to his nieces one day. He knew I'd be a sweet, loving mother. I'll say I knew about him when he sent me a love letter shortly after his father was diagnosed with a brain tumor. He was a peanut M&M – hard coating on the outside, but soft, sweet, and a little nutty on the inside.

So I kissed the frog and he became my prince and blah, blah, blah. Sweet story.

Now, I hope feminists don't send me hate mail, but I've always kind of romanticized the whole "knight-in-shining-armor" thing. The notion of someone taking care of me was appealing back then. Ah, yes, I know, I was a twenty-something-year-old fool. This man, whom I will henceforth refer to as Hubby, promised me a lot of things – a nice life, a big house, travel, and lots of babies with whom I could play house.

Yep, I was all set to be a "kept" woman, someone who needed someone to take care of her. And nothing spelled this out more than an incident that happened on our honeymoon in Mexico.

I suggested to Hubby that we leave our all-inclusive resort for a day and travel inland to the pyramids at Chichén Itzá. Being an elementary school teacher, I wanted to experience this slice of Mayan history myself. Hubby, however, just wanted to stay at the resort and keep ordering "una cerveza más" so he could get his money's worth out of our trip (plus that was all the culture he really wanted anyway).

But he relented and off we set in a bus with substandard air-conditioning on a journey toward Central American history. Now, the concierge at the resort assured us this was a four-hour trip – tops – and we'd be back to the resort by lunchtime.

## I Just Want to Be Alone

We're still not sure how he could have been so wrong about that. And for the record, thirteen years later, Hubby is still pissed that we lost a whole day of "all-inclusive" eating and drinking at the resort.

After about three stops in tiny Mexican villages along the way – to buy souvenirs and have a lunch of sketchy brown chicken and yellow water – we finally reached the ruins of Chichén Itzá. The main pyramid, El Castillo, was large and impressive. I noticed that people were climbing it, and despite my paralyzing fear of heights, I somehow thought ascending this seventy-eight foot tall structure would be a good idea.

"Race you up!" I called to Hubby and started pulling myself up the narrow stairway by the single rope running up the middle of the steps.

"Hey, wait, that's really high up and you don't … " Hubby started, but then ran up after me.

Once I got to the top I turned around and almost lost my balance. Shit. We were high. And there were no railings or barricades because, you know, Mexico circa 2001.

I backed up against the temple at the center of the pyramid and plastered myself against the wall.

"Wow, this is so cool!" Hubby was walking around all four sides of the pyramid, clearly not concerned about how close he was to the edge. "You can see for miles up here."

"Get over here!" I hissed, "You're going to fall, and I'm going to be a widow."

He laughed – laughed! – and continued to gaze out at the Yucatán Peninsula.

I found an opening to the inner temple chamber and planted myself next to the cool wall, breathing heavily. Screw the scenery, I was scared shitless!

"Hey, Sweetie, we better head down," Hubby popped his head in. "There's lightening and it's starting to rain."

I slid my feet out slowly and caught my breath. Shit. We were high. And there were no railings or anything to hold on our way down. Plus the stairs were like, four inches wide. Damn, those ancient Mayans had some tiny-ass feet.

*Flash. Crack.* Shit.

"How in the hell am I going to get down?!?" I screeched at Hubby, who was looking rather amused. I would have kicked him in the nuts, but I couldn't move my feet. "I am going to die a virgin up here. This is where they sacrificed virgins, you know."

"You're thirty-one. You haven't been a virgin in a long time, Honey," Hubby said offhandedly as he walked from one side of the pyramid to the other. "Here's what we're going to do," his voice was as gentle as if he were talking to a child, "we're going to scoot down on our butts. I'll go first, you sit right behind me, and we'll hold the rope."

After twenty-three "I can'ts!" and twenty-four "You have tos" because the lightening was getting really close, we scooted our way down El Castillo and back on to the bus, arriving back at the resort by about ten o'clock that night. We promptly proceeded to drink our way into comas – he because he had to make up for lost "all-inclusive" time and me because I didn't die.

We hardly ever speak of the time he rescued me from certain death, but he chides me about it anytime we are near a railing or someplace high. It's just what he does.

So my Frog Prince and I settled into our happy married life that soon included a little brick fixer-upper, fertility shots, and at long last, babies.

Lots of babies, just like ~~I wanted~~ we discussed.

Right out of the gate he was a wonderful, involved father. He had to be because we were blessed with twins. It was perfect man-to-man defense until the third came barreling along a mere seventeen months later and a fourth two years after that.

As if four little boys under the age of five weren't overwhelming enough, one of our twins was diagnosed with an inoperable brain tumor and died when he was in kindergarten. Through it all, Hubby was my savior again, talking to doctors so I wouldn't have to, and e-mailing dozens of hospitals around the country because I couldn't, and patiently waiting until I could talk about any of it.

The storm eventually passed and lo and behold, we were blessed with a fifth little boy.

And suddenly, I was tired and needed a break.

My sister was getting remarried and having a bridal shower. The kicker was that it was three hours away, and I would be spending the night. I offered to take the boys with me, to which Hubby paused just a few seconds too long *(bastard)* before saying, "No, you go enjoy yourself. The boys and I will be fine."

I started to leave an extensive list of instructions like names, birthdates, identifying birthmarks, social security numbers, and allergies, not to mention food preferences, sleeping patterns, and bathroom habits, but Hubby dismissed all of this.

"And I didn't have time to fold the boys' church pants, so they are still in the dryer. You'll have to get those out and . . ." I stopped short of saying, *"fold them"* because really, was I expecting miracles?

"Really, I got this!" He said in his best George Lopez imitation. "We will be fine. They're my kids. I think I know how to take care of them." He gave me a patronizing kiss and sent me on my way.

I was feeling pretty bad the whole drive. Maybe he didn't really need me. It was clear *I needed him* for so many things, but what did *he need me* for? I imagined all the boys laughing and having a wonderful time, not missing me at all. "Mom? What mom? Who's that? Parrrtay!"

I had a great time with my mom, my sister, and her friends at the shower, but I was really anxious to get home the next day. I walked in the house, expecting four little boys to knock me over with kisses and hugs and my wonderful husband to present me with the biggest bouquet of flowers the market had on hand.

Instead, silence – eerie, yet oddly messy, silence greeted me. I walked in the kitchen and saw microwave popcorn bags and empty cracker boxes all over the counter. Half of the church pants were in a basket in the living room and the other half was still hanging out of the open dryer. Blankets and toys littered the family room. Dirty dishes were in the sink and clean dishes were in the dishwasher.

Upstairs, more blankets, stuffed animals, and lovies littered our bed and floor.

I sighed, as I parked my suitcase next to the wall. I got to work cleaning up the house – putting the boys' things away, cleaning the kitchen, and retrieving the rest of the pants from the dryer.

Soon enough, the door slammed and a rush of little boys came pouring in, "MOOOMMMYYY!! YOU'RE HOME!!!"

Then it was hugs and "I missed you" and "How was your weekend?"

And that's when the tattling began. Not on each other, but on Hubby.

"Daddy couldn't get Edgie into his crib so he just let him fall asleep on the floor in his room," the eight-year-old began. "We all slept in here because Daddy was watching a basketball game and wouldn't tuck us in."

The boys nodded in agreement. "Mom, we didn't eat a single vegetable all weekend long!" The eight-year-old continued excitedly. I gave a sidelong glance at Hubby. He was looking sheepish.

"We didn't really eat at home," the five-year-old chimed in. "We went out to eat with Grandma last night, and tonight we went over to Aunt Donna's."

I looked full-on at Hubby this time. "What? She was having Sunday family dinner," he grinned.

"Did you go to church?" I asked the boys sweetly.

"Yeah," answered the eight-year-old again quickly. "We picked up Grandma, and then she took us out to breakfast."

"What did you wear?" At this point, I imagined them all traipsing into church like a bunch of rag-a-muffins still wearing pajamas with Coco Puffs stuck to them.

"Dad made us wear our nice pants," the six-year-old whined.

"Yeah, but Edgie had to get them for Dad!" The ten-year-old finally spoke up.

I rounded on Hubby. "You had to have the two-year-old tell you whose pants were whose?"

"Well, he knew! And he wanted to help," Hubby answered defensively.

"Umm hmmm," I clucked. "Anything else go on? Did you get your homework done for Monday, Slim?"

"Yeah, but Dad had to call Aunt Maureen to help with my English because she used to be a teacher like you, Mom."

"Dad didn't really know what he was doing, Mom," said the eight-year-old, under Hubby's disapproving gaze.

Hubby pulled me close into a hug. "We really missed you. Nobody can take care of these kids – and me – like you can. I don't know what we'd do without you."

What a ~~bullshitter~~ smooth talker. I've never felt so needed in my entire life.

I guess sometimes the knight-in-shining armor needs saving, too.


*KATHY GLOW is a freelance writer, blogger, and mother of five boys, including one lost to cancer. When she is not driving all over town in her mini-van, wiping "boy stuff" off the walls, or trying to find the bottom of the pile of laundry, she writes about what life is really like after all your dreams come true on her blog, kissing the frog. A 2013 BlogHer Voices of the Year Honoree, she is also a regular contributor to Mamalode.com. Her writing has been featured on BlogHer, Huffington Post Parents, Her View from Home, and Mamapedia. She is also one of the contributing authors to* Sunshine After the Storm: A Survival Guide for the Grieving Mother.

# My Husband's Visit to the Gynecologist
## By Bethany Meyer
### *I Love Them the Most When They're Sleeping*

Am I in the minority when I boast that my husband had his parts glued back together by a gynecologist?

Why? Because everything in our house is a production.

I am married to David. And David loves his projects. He needs to be immersed in something. If a project by definition is something in which one is immersed, then I've been David's project on four different occasions. Because we have four children together. All sons. I think a project is a healthy outlet for David. So long as those projects don't interfere with the well-being of the kids we already have and provided they don't impregnate me with any more, I love his projects too.

It works out best when he focuses on them one project at a time.

His urgent visit to the gynecologist was the result of two projects colliding.

Because everything in our house is a production.

I'll call project one Operation Fastest 5K.

David is a ridiculous athlete. Most times I say that with pride. Occasionally I mutter it with a mix of annoyance and disgust. When we first met, he scheduled his weekends around when and where the most competitive pickup games were played at the basketball courts on the Jersey shore. As we've gotten older, he's become increasingly frustrated playing basketball. He's either frustrated that his body can't do what it used to, or frustrated that other players are "playing like a bunch of fucking pussies." *His words. Not mine.*

This irritation with basketball is what led him to running.

I love running. Like LOVE love it. I didn't always love it. It was an acquired taste, like beer. Now that I'm an adult, as much as I love a cold beer I actually prefer a good run.   Sometimes I run to train for races. Other times, I run simply to train for life. I enjoy getting lost on trail runs. I dig intervals at the track. But nothing compares to a long, slow run with an unlikely partner who matches your labored gait stride for stride, sees you at your most vulnerable, finds a clean leaf for you to wipe with when you have to poop unexpectedly in the woods, and becomes your dear friend and close confidante as a result.

David enjoys every aspect of the running puzzle except for the elusive … and I deem essential … running partner piece.

"You should run with someone," I suggest.

"That's a waste of my time," he claims.

"It makes it more fun," I offer.

"It's not supposed to be fun," he admonishes.

"It helps you run farther," I say.

"I go far enough by myself," he argues.

"It will challenge you to run faster," I say.

"Not unless I can find someone faster than I am," he replies.

*Which isn't exactly a "no."*

So, that is my mission. To find someone faster than David.

It takes me awhile, but I find him. Dante. The father of one of our third son's classmates. Thinner, younger, and faster than David. The only question remaining is whether or not their personalities will mesh. David elicits strong emotions in people. They either REALLY like him or REALLY dislike him. For the bromance to work, I need them to gel. And I need this bromance to work. When I learn that Dante will be accompanying his son to a classmate's birthday party, I elect David to take our son.

"Now, listen, the guy I want to hook you up with will be there," I remind him.

"What?"

"Your future running partner," I reply as I straighten the collar on his golf shirt.

He rolls his eyes, "I don't need a running partner."

"Yes, you do. It's the missing piece of the puzzle for you. Just try not to offend him."

He looks stunned, "What does that mean?"

I wag my finger at him, "You know what it means. Don't be all, 'I bet I could win *Survivor*' with him. You would never win *Survivor* because people find your personality offensive at times. Especially during a competitive situation. So, don't offend him. I want this relationship to work."

He returns home from the party wearing a smile and proudly displaying the digits. They are already text buddies. With a scheduled run on the calendar.

Like the medieval parent who has orchestrated an arranged marriage, I worry about the match the first month they run together.

*What have I done? Did I push this on them? Is it too soon? Should they have courted longer? Will it backfire on all of us and we'll eventually avoid one another at school?*

But, I'm thrilled to report, a year later, the bromance is stronger than ever. They're equally competitive and equally obsessed with each other. They are a perfect fit.

Operation Fastest 5K has been a year in the making. Dante runs with David, designs his training schedule, and is on the receiving end of his numerous phone calls...some nervous, most excited. David executes the training schedule. And I love watching the pieces of the running puzzle fit together perfectly for him as my husband continues to set and exceed his running goals.

The son of a bitch is fast.

\*       \*       \*

Now for some background on Project Two.

I'll call it Operation Backyard Garden.

"I think we should have a garden," he says one day.

"Great," I agree.

"I'm serious about this. I want the kids involved," he warns.

"OK," I repeat.

He's not finished, "Think about how great it will be to plant things and watch them grow. Then eat them."

"I'm on board!" I say with a smile.

*You don't have to keep selling me. Also, your children don't eat vegetables.*

He puts his hands on his hips, "I'm going to have to research this. I want to do it properly."

I raise my eyebrows and nod, "Naturally."

Because David is all about the research. Years ago, a friend invited him to play racquetball. David had never picked up a racquet, but was confident his athletic prowess would secure him a win. Imagine his surprise when he lost. *I secretly loved it.* Smarting from the defeat, he drove directly from the racquetball court to the library, borrowed a book about racquetball, read it from cover to cover, and then demanded a rematch. He redeemed himself by handing his buddy a good old fashioned smack down.

Within a day of making his garden declaration, a stack of books from the library occupies a section of the kitchen counter. Fruits, vegetables, flowers, vines, bushes ... all things gardening. Evidence that he is serious about his threat to begin to garden.

He debates how he'll plant the garden. Then finally settles on boxes. We have labored discussions about where to place the boxes.

"Let's get rid of the swing set," he suggests.

Our second born son overhears him and interjects, "What? We use the swing set!"

He explains to our boy, "That's where the best light is. You're going to have to sacrifice the swing set for these vegetables."

"I don't even like vegetables!" the child exclaims.

I intervene gently, "That's a big undertaking ... dismantling the swing set. A lot of work. And the kids do use the swing set." I scour the yard and point to an area close to the house. "How about over there?"

He immediately shakes his head. "No. No light over there in the morning."

I look around and point to another spot that borders the yard, "How about over there?"

He sighs. He frowns. He hems. He haws. "Maybe. I'll have to take out that lilac tree." He approaches the area as he extracts the tape measure from his tool belt. "I'll watch the light in this space today. Which irritates me because I already built the boxes, and I really wanted to get a jump on getting them set up and getting the soil prepped." He shakes his head again. "I'm going to check on my plants."

His plants have been growing on the top shelf in my laundry room, under twenty-four hour fluorescent light bulbs, for four weeks. The top shelf in my laundry room is usually home to the paper towels and toilet paper. They've been temporarily relocated to the top of the washer and dryer. And, since they are all round, they roll off the washer and dryer during their cycles. And since we have four children, the washer and dryer are running at all hours. Which means the laundry room floor has been littered with paper towels and toilet paper rolls for the past month.

*But soon we'll have vegetables, right?*

Early the next morning, David rises and takes inventory of the light situation on the proposed gardening plot. Miraculously he approves. Immediately he begins digging. He's done his homework down to the soil, which is a mix of compost, peat moss, and vermiculite. When he regales me with tales about it, this means nothing to me. When I overhear him laughing as he tells my cousin that people shy away from vermiculite because it was rumored to have components of asbestos in it, I start paying closer attention.

*Rumored? And we'll be consuming the vegetables that grow in the soil that* may *have asbestos in it? Is his life insurance paid up?*

I've got some research of my own to do.

So, he lays his possibly lethal combo in each of the four custom made garden boxes. And he maneuvers his feet around the paper towels and toilet paper to tend to his plants growing on the top shelf in my laundry room.

One evening, with a clap of his hands and a twinkle in his eye, he announces, "I'm almost ready to plant them. The last thing I need to do is create the lattice squares that will define the area for every plant in its box. Like a tic-tac-toe board, only with more squares."

I'm half listening as I nod in agreement, "Mm hmm."

He continues, "I'll get started on them, but I have to get to bed early because I have my 5K race tomorrow, and I'm really hoping to run it in my goal time."

"Mm hmm," I say, still half listening, now half nodding.

He heads outside to use the little bit of remaining daylight to play around with the wood and take measurements for the boxes.

In bed that night, David heaves his body from side to side, seemingly unable to find a comfortable position. But I know better. The night before a race is always accompanied by restless sleep. And this night is no exception. He has a full blown case of pre-race jitters.

After seven hours of fitful semi-sleep, his feet hit the floor at five in the morning. With one bloodshot eye half-open, I watch him exit the bedroom. Then I listen to his feet make contact with every squeaky board on his descent downstairs. *Like a moth to a flame.*

The last thing I hear before falling back to sleep is the sound of the back door opening.

*He's gone outside to the garden …*

*       *       *

And this is the point of impact.

Operation Backyard Garden crashes into Operation Fastest 5K.

I sense a presence in the bedroom and open my eyes suddenly.

David is pacing back and forth in our bedroom. He's holding his right hand up by his face. He turns his head to look at me, and I'm immediately blinded by light. He's wearing a headlamp. I hear a click signaling he's turned it off. I blink twice and open my eyes again. There is blood dripping down his arm. Lots of blood.

"I think I'm out for the race! Do you fucking believe this?" he says in a strained voice.

Dumbfounded and half asleep, I ask, "What's happening?"

"I need you to look at my finger," he demands.

"What's wrong with your finger?"

"I cut it," he explains, "I need you to look at it."

"You cut it with what?" I inquire.

"This!" He keeps his bleeding arm at eye level and uses his left hand to raise the instrument in question up for me to see.

## I Love Them the Most When They're Sleeping

*Sweet mother of God.*

He brandishes a handsaw with the sharpest, most jagged teeth I've ever seen. There is crimson blood on the blade in one area. It's like peering into the mouth of a great white shark.

"What the hell is that? Get that thing out of the bedroom before the kids wake up and see it!" I say furiously.

He lays it on the bed. "It's a wood saw. I couldn't sleep because of the race. So, I went outside to create the lattice boxes for the garden. It's still dark outside." He points at his head. "That's why I'm wearing my headlamp. I was trying to be considerate and not use my electrical tools so early in the morning. The saw slipped as I was cutting a piece of wood. And it went right into my index finger and thumb!"

He brings his hand closer for me to inspect.

"ACK!!" I whisper in protest, "You know I have a weak stomach! I can't look at that! I'll pass out!"

He pulls his hand back, "I know! I'm sorry, but I think I need stitches. This is totally going to fuck me for my race, I just know it!"

I frown. "I'd be more concerned about getting a tetanus shot!"

"Shit, I didn't even think about that," he mutters.

"That saw doesn't scream tetanus shot at you?"

"Can you just please look at it?" he pleads.

I shake my head. "NO! Go wake the oldest! He is great with blood and gore!"

"Good idea," he agrees.

I know I'm a total wuss, but I do not do well with anything deeper than a paper cut. Our oldest son can take inventory of the situation.

David leaves the bedroom.

And quickly returns.

"He won't wake up. I'm sorry, I hate to ask, but I think you have to look at it," he says as he brings his hand closer to me.

"NO! Just wait! Let me think! The neighbor down the street is a nurse. She'll look at it. She'll know if you need stitches." *And a tetanus shot.*

"Good idea. I'll be right back."

I know. I'm awful. But I don't do deep wounds.

Or broken bones.

He leaves the house.

And quickly returns.

He is in a full panic, "She wasn't there. You're my only hope! Please, can you just look at it?"

I push myself up to a seated position. Place a pillow behind my head. Take a deep breath. *I hate being the Mom sometimes.* "Fine, I'll look at it."

He places his index finger close to my face for inspection. And I gag down the vomit that threatens to make an appearance.

*Oh boy. That's deep.*

"You need stitches," I relay. *And a tetanus shot.*

He places the fingers of his left hand on either side of the gash and proceeds to open and close it repeatedly. It looks like a bloody mouth opening and closing.

I push his arm away from me and put my head between my legs. "Why did you do that?" I demand.

"Do what?" he asks, miffed.

"Why did you open and close it like that? I think I saw the bone! You know I can't handle blood!"

"Sorry. So, you think I need stitches?" he asks.

"Yes!" *And a tetanus shot!*

He's back to pacing. "Great. Just great. I'm fucked for this race. If I go to the hospital, we'll never get to the race on time. What should we do?"

My head remains between my legs while I take deep breaths.

I tell him, "I'm going to pick my head up, but please don't show me that gaping wound again." I raise my head and look tentatively in his direction. His finger is covered, and he is still pacing. I continue, "If we call our pediatrician friends, they will most certainly send us to the hospital for a tetanus shot and stitches."

"I'd like to avoid going to the hospital," he states.

"OK. How about we text our friend, Dr. Jay?" I offer.

"The gynecologist?" he inquires.

I nod. "Yes."

He frowns. "I didn't cut my vagina. I cut my finger."

*Well, that's debatable.*

I nod again. "Yes, but maybe we can send him a picture of your finger, and see if he thinks you need stitches." *And a tetanus shot.*

"Good thinking." he looks around. "The light is terrible in here. The sun has just come up, so I'll take a picture with my phone outside," he says as he exits the room.

I look at the clock on my nightstand. It's just after seven on Saturday morning.

*Jesus Christ Almighty. Why is everything in this house a production?*

Wild-eyed, David returns to the bedroom. "OK, I took a video."

*Say what?*

I am so confused. "A video? Why a video?"

"Well, then he can get a better perspective," he explains.

*Why, yes, the four kids combined ARE easier than their father, why do you ask?*

I shake my head. "Just send it to me so that I can forward it to Mrs. Jay."

I type this message to Mrs. Jay:

David cut his right index finger above his knuckle this A.M. Not making me breakfast, this was a gardening accident. It's deep enough that it probably needs a stitch. Or glue. It's in a spot that bends a lot. I think he wants to butterfly it closed, but he cut it on a serrated saw. So I worry he may need a tetanus shot. Is Dr. Jay around that he can look at this video and weigh in? Hospital or no?

I attach the video, which is footage of David bending his finger repeatedly at the knuckle. While the birds chirp merrily in the background.

I hit "send" and suffer through a wave of douchebag chills.

I look at David. "I feel like a tool bothering them on a Saturday morning."

He holds up his mangled finger in response. "I know, but this is an emergency."

*Of your own making,* I think as my phone rings suddenly.

# I Just Want to Be Alone

I answer, "Hello?"

"It's Mrs. Jay. Just send him over and the Doc will stitch him up. We were on our way to Starbucks. We'll wait."

We love Dr. and Mrs. Jay.

"Thank you and we totally owe you," I say before we hang up.

Twenty minutes later, she texts me a picture of our husbands with their heads hunched over her kitchen counter. Neither of them has brushed his hair or shaved. And the good Doctor appears to be gluing David's finger back together. Unless this is frowned upon by our HMO. In which case, this is a purely fictional story.

Mrs. Jay writes, "The Doc just gave David a two for one deal … Dermabond and a Pap smear."

Did I mention we love Dr. and Mrs. Jay?

I'm relieved to find the handsaw on my kitchen counter. Thus, he did not bring it with him for a medical version of Saturday morning show-and-tell with the gynecologist.

David returns within the hour. His wound is clean, and the glue appears to be holding. He resumes pacing … this time in nervous anticipation of his afternoon race.

We make it to the race just before the gun signals the start. After a year's worth of hard work, my husband exceeds the goal he set for himself. And on a very hilly course to boot. And I say it proudly, without an ounce of annoyance or disgust. I capture a shot of him crossing the finish line with his finish time, a personal record, in bright lights alongside him. Knowing his running partner and closest confidante is eager to hear his results, I post it immediately to Facebook.

The kids and I rush toward him to offer congratulatory hugs and wide smiles.

He gasps for air, and asks me, "Dante? Did you text him?"

The bond runs deep between running partners.

I smile. "Already on Facebook. He will know soon enough."

Another huge production. But a day we won't soon forget.

David's garden is growing nicely. We'll have green beans that none of our children will consume before the month is over.

The bromance continues.
And his wound is healing beautifully.
I can't help but think when I look at it though ...
It looks exactly like a vagina.

*BETHANY MEYER lives in Philadelphia with her husband and their four sons. No, they will not be trying for a girl. Bethany's chapter, "Parenting is Taboo", was published in the best-selling anthology I Just Want to Pee Alone. Brain, Child Magazine will publish Bethany's original chapter in their book This is Childhood in late spring, 2014. Bethany is a contributor to an anthology compiled by Another Mother Runner, which will be published in July, 2014. She is also a contributing writer at WhatToExpect.com, and her work has been featured on The Huffington Post. While the sippy cup days are safely behind her, the sexting days loom forebodingly ahead. She laments this on her blog, I Love Them the Most When They're Sleeping.*

## Showcase *This*
## By Janel Mills
### *649.133: Girls, the Care and Maintenance Of*

My husband, Rob, doesn't have it easy. He lives in a house full of females. His only male ally is the dog, who would sell him out in a hot minute for a forgotten low-lying bowl of cereal. He's been growing his chest-length beard for five years and insists that he is the inspiration for the current beard craze (he also claims he is responsible for the pea coat craze of the early 2000s). His favorite pastime is watching shitty seventies-era horror movies in the basement. Some people would describe him as cynical, but he would tell you he's a realist. He has a low tolerance for bullshit and isn't afraid to tell you to fuck off if he thinks you deserve it.

He is not exactly the target marketing demographic for Disney.

Last year, I informed my husband that we would be spending part of our income tax refund on a trip to Disney World. Our oldest daughter, who was five at the time, was obsessed with the idea of going, and I was tired of telling her no. Rob, who enjoys traveling about as much as he enjoys thinking about making his vasectomy appointment, reluctantly agreed. So we went. And you know what? That advertising CD Disney sends you when they hear you're thinking about possibly booking a trip? It doesn't lie. Disney World was every bit as magical, wonderful and downright charming as you imagine it to be. Even Rob had to agree that he didn't have a constant, overwhelming urge to go back to the air-conditioned hotel room and watch basic cable the majority of the trip.

Then we went to the World Showcase at Epcot.

For those who aren't familiar with this particular circle of hell, allow me to explain: the World Showcase is basically an enormous collection of internationally-themed gift shops that your kids have zero interest in visiting. You won't realize this, though, until you get to the Japan pavilion, which is halfway around the lake, leaving you no choice but to soldier on through the rest of the nations. I am seriously convinced that there is a secret underground club run by Disney that commissions people to convince tourists to visit the

World Showcase. I can't tell you how many people told me to visit this specific part of Epcot Center with my kids. Everything I read about it told me that they would not enjoy it. But anytime I expressed my doubts, these people would begin preaching the Gospel of the World Showcase. If you were one of these people, let me make my feelings clear: you are either terribly mistaken about what kids enjoy or you purposely tried to make me have a bad time at Disney World, in which case you are a complete asshole.

So there we were, wandering around the World Showcase on our last day of the trip. It was so goddamn hot that day. The kids were exhausted from walking, and Rob and I were exhausted from carrying two forty-pound kids who'd given up on walking two days prior. We finally made it to the final and most infuriating pavilion, *The American Adventure*, which doesn't even attempt to disguise the fact that it's just a regular gift shop like the one in the lobby of your hotel. As Rob pointed out the exit, we approached a gazebo with a sign that read, "Meet Duffy here!" Sure enough, there stood Duffy, or rather, a person in a bear costume no doubt sweating their ass off and questioning the choices they had made in life that had led them to this point.

Duffy, for the record, is a made-up character that isn't attached to a movie, TV show, or video game. It's just a teddy bear only sold in Disney World gift shops. Once you own the bear, you have the privilege of purchasing additional outfits for Duffy. I have to imagine that in terms of the character costume totem pole, Duffy is the costume reserved for the newbies and the fuckups who can't be relied on to show up for work.

What's that you say? You've never heard of Duffy? That's OK, neither had my kids, but that didn't stop them from insisting they *had* to meet him. There were signs all over the place in Epcot, and apparently they had done their job because there we were, standing in line to meet Duffy.

"Thank God it's a short line," I said to my husband. The instant I said those words, the Duffy handlers announced that Duffy had to take a quick break, and would be back in twenty minutes. We were behind one person when they announced this. "Girls, if we want to meet Duffy, we'll have to stand here and wait for twenty minutes. Do you really want to meet Duffy?" Yes, of course they did. So we sat in that gazebo watching our kids run around like idiots waiting to take their picture with a fake character that neither of them will remember in a year.

I looked over at my husband after about ten minutes, and I could see that his real-o-meter was slowly creeping into the red. After spending the day walking around in the Florida heat wearing his usual uniform of a black T-shirt and jeans, wrangling cranky, irrational kids while dealing with crowds of strangers and morons, he was feeling less than magical. He couldn't even daydream about the air-conditioned hotel room because we'd already checked out in anticipation of our trip home that day. The Duffy Situation was becoming critical.

Finally, Duffy and his handlers came back from their smoke break, and I'm not kidding, my kids went nuts. You would have thought this was the entire reason we brought them to Disney. My middle daughter, who refused to go anywhere near the majority of characters we saw during our trip, gave Duffy a fucking hug and flashed the biggest smile in the history of camera smiles. It was ridiculous. Rob and I couldn't even believe the level of bullshit we were witnessing. After three failed attempts at taking a picture where everyone is looking forward with their eyes open, our turn with Duffy was over. It was time to get the fuck out of the World Showcase and Florida in general.

Rob began herding the girls down the ramp to exit the gazebo, passing the other hard-core Duffy fans still waiting in line. That was when he dropped a line that I've heard a million times at home, but never in public, and certainly not in The Happiest Place on Earth. Rob hurried the girls along, and as he did so, he said, "Come on, dickheads, let's go."

Oh yes, he did.

"Dickheads" is Rob's pet name for the kids when they're being annoying. However, Rob doesn't usually use this charming nickname for the kids while walking past a line full of strangers. When I heard him loudly encouraging my darling dickheads to get moving, I looked up at the two young teenage girls who had been standing in line behind us for the past twenty minutes. They were frozen in fear and staring at Rob, no doubt wracking their brain trying to figure out what they had done to make the tall bearded man so angry. When I noticed the frightened look on their faces, I realized what they were thinking.

"Oh no, not you," I said with a reassuring smile. "He was talking to the kids."

I actually said that.

Oh yes, I did.

I said it with a great big "glad we got that straightened out!" smile. When the expression on the teenagers' faces changed from fear to "wait, what?", I hit rewind on what I had just said and realized I hadn't really helped matters. I decided to skip trying to explain myself and my husband's choice in words to a couple of fourteen-year-olds and instead hopped on the Dickhead Train that was choo choo-ing quickly down the track and towards the exit for the Shittiest Place on Earth.

I didn't need to explain myself to those girls. What was there to explain? So he called his five- and three-year-old daughters "dickheads." Big fucking deal. My kids don't even know what a dick *is*, so it certainly didn't matter to them. They don't care about Rob using words in front of them that their friends' parents would never dream of using. They don't care that Rob's never going to be the dad at Disney World wearing the Goofy hat and matching family T-shirt, or that tea parties and Barbie sessions aren't really his thing. They honestly couldn't give a shit about any of those things. Rob is Daddy, and Daddy is the coolest person on Earth as far as they're concerned. He is who he is, and that's why we love him. He doesn't need to censor himself in any way for us. We love him just as R-rated as he is, and he loves us with a fierce loyalty that you don't see every day. That guy would do damn near anything to make us happy.

Except go back to the World Showcase. Fuck that place.

## I Just Want to Be Alone

*JANEL MILLS is the librarian/thug behind the blog <u>649.133: Girls, the Care and Maintenance Of</u>, where she writes about raising a princess, a wild child, and the happiest toddler on Earth using as many curse words as possible. Janel is a contributor to <u>NickMom</u>, and has also been featured on <u>In the Powder Room</u>, Scary Mommy, and was a contributor to the wildly successful anthology "You Have Lipstick On Your Teeth." Check out her periodically neglected <u>Facebook</u> page or her hilarious but universally ignored <u>Twitter</u> feed. When not blogging or librarian-ing, she keeps busy raising three beautiful little girls with her beardedly gifted husband in the wilds of metro Detroit.*

# Dads Make Good Babysitters. (No They Don't.)
## By Rebecca Gallagher
### *Frugalista Blog*

I'm totally kidding about the title of this post. Dads aren't babysitters. They are parents. They parent their kids the same way as the mother parents the children.

*<crickets, crickets>*

Okay, maybe not THE SAME. But you know, kinda the same. Like they feed them a meal that's nutritious and satisfying while you are off doing the grocery shopping and getting a haircut. The meal might be goldfish crackers and fruit by the foot, but hey, it IS food. So, there's that.

When my husband was first left alone with our eldest it was when she was an infant around six months. Now hold the phone. My husband had been left alone with her before. But not at bedtime. This was sacred territory. My daughter was still nursing and her night-time nurse session with me was very important to get her to settle down. Nothing else worked. She drank from a bottle during the day-time but it wasn't the same when it came to night time.

I had an outing with my mom and a friend that night. We had tickets to the opera for my friend's fortieth birthday. My friend was going through chemo for breast cancer and I wanted to really treat her to a special outing. My husband was a great sport and knew this meant a lot to me.

So off I went to the opera. I left explicit instructions for him with a bottle of expressed milk; the baby's jammies on the changing table and whatever else that might help. I think I left a sweater or shirt that I had worn that day in her crib so that she would have my smell near her. I read that somewhere and figured it was worth a shot.

It felt so good to go out in the evening with other adults. I was wary leaving the baby but for heaven's sakes, it's her dad. He's fine! Piece of cake.

The opera was lovely, I only fell asleep once. Dinner was delicious, and my friend enjoyed herself. I returned home sometime around eleven that night and much to my delight, the baby was sleeping in her crib.

# I Just Want to Be Alone

Oh my goodness! Everything went beautifully! I peeked in on Emma. She was wearing her yellow fleece jammies just like I put out. I tiptoed away and dare not go near her room after that.

First born babies are nerve wracking. You hold your breath at every stir and flinch, and heaven forbid they wake up and need soothing. I mean, of course they do! And you jump at every little murmur they make. Forget basic needs like emptying your bladder first or getting on pants. Second babies are easy. You are much more relaxed and deaf to the minutia of all their stirring. You wait for them to wail at the top of their lungs and then drag yourself to their crib side.

So off to bed I went that night. I'm sure I thanked hubs for a great job. He said it was a piece of cake and she didn't fuss at all. Took her bottle and snuggled and then fell asleep. I wasn't going to even let a thought sneak in my head that I felt a pang of sadness for her NOT missing me. NOPE. This was a good thing. A good thing indeed.

Just like routine, she awoke sometime that early morning for another feeding. Probably around four or so. I used to nurse her and then fall asleep on the spare bed we had in her room. We tried sleep training her and we did pretty well. If pretty well means rocking your child to sleep, laying them in the crib like Indiana Jones replacing an ancient relic on a pedestal and then tip toeing out of that room hoping the boulder doesn't come rolling after you. The boulder is a metaphor for the child waking up, by the way, if you needed that explained.

She would sleep just fine for a few hours on her own until she woke up and I came in to nurse her back to sleep. Okay, yes, I realize that isn't sleep training. But these are the mistakes first time parents make. We thought this was working. And it was – to a point.

Okay, so back to that morning. I brought her to me in the spare bed and nursed her. I fell asleep, like usual. Then we both awoke sometime that morning around seven or eight. I can't remember exactly. I nursed her again, I'm sure.

I noticed her pajamas seemed damp. It was as if she was sweating through the flame retardant polyester footed pajamas. Oh my gosh! Did she have a fever? She seemed warm-ish. But then, she'd been snuggled next to me in the bed. I felt her cheeks and head. She seemed normal to me. Why was she so damp? Her whole front and back side of her jammies were moist and felt almost sweaty.

I brought her to the changing table to change her nighttime diaper. I placed her on the table, I unzipped her jammies, and well, HI THERE!

I FOUND THAT SHE WASN'T WEARING A DIAPER!

She wasn't sweaty, she was soaking in her own urine!! Oh, good Lord!

I called to my husband to come into the room. He was already up getting the tea and coffee ready.

I TRIED not to sound condescending when I asked, "Did you forget anything when you tucked in Emma last night? Because something doesn't look right here."

I displayed the babe's feminine folds and creases exposed under her jammies. What should be a puffy front section of plastic Pampers was instead chubby, naked baby flesh.

"Huh. I thought I put a diaper on her." He casually walks away back to the kitchen.

Oh right! Just act all natural about it. In my head I'm going like this, *What the eff?*

How do you put pajamas on a naked baby ass? How? I ask you!

My concerns over a potential fever quickly were replaced with the realization that I had been snuggling a bag of polyester urine.

Those pajamas were so absorbent that the mattress wasn't even damp.

Bless my husband's heart. He was so concerned with getting Emma settled, I think his flustered state made him forget the diaper.

In the end, it didn't matter anyway. Emma didn't seem bothered. After that trial run, I got to have a night out here and there with a friend and the husband was solid in his dad duties.

So no, my husband doesn't 'babysit' his daughter. Of course not.

## I Just Want to Be Alone

He parents her. A babysitter would remember the diaper.

*REBECCA GALLAGHER is a SAHM to a teenager and tweenager. A recovering aspiring actress, she laughs at herself on a daily basis. She writes at her blog, Frugalista Blog, which isn't about couponing. She likes movies, Daniel Craig, tea and makeup. She can be found driving her minivan to PTA meetings and heading to Target in yoga pants and cashmere. She spends too much time on Pinterest checking beauty tips and not enough time cleaning her house. You can find her on Facebook and Twitter @FrugieBlog. She's proud to be a part of the two best-selling humor anthologies,* I Just Want to Pee Alone *and* "You Have Lipstick On Your Teeth." *Rebecca is Bedroom Editor at Bonbon Break, has been featured on Babble, In the Powder Room, and Scary Mommy and was a one-time parent blog of the week on Huff Post.*

# BJs, Ball Punches, and Mayonnaise
## By Nicole Knepper
### *Moms Who Drink and Swear*

**Eric:** Where are you?

**Me:** I'm on the way to the grocery store.

**Eric:** Still? You left like, a long time ago.

**Me:** I left like, ten minutes ago.

**Eric:** Feels like forever. I miss you.

**Me:** No you don't. What do you want?

**Eric:** Mayonnaise. We are out. And I want a blowjob.

**Me:** We are not out. I want you to look carefully. It's there!

**Eric:** I did look. We don't have any. You haven't given me a blowjob for like, a long time.

**Me:** OH MY GOD! I SWEAR WE HAVE MAYONNAISE! And I gave you a blowjob, like yesterday or the day before.

**Eric:** It was a week ago. And we have no mayo. Get some, okay?

**Me:** No, I won't get some, because we have some. I will punch you in the balls instead of giving you a blowjob if you don't stop bothering me. Move stuff around and LOOK FOR IT. It's there.

**Eric:** I DID LOOK! And when you get home and see that there's no mayonnaise, you will give me a blowjob.

**Me:** Deal. Because I know we have some. I'm looking forward to punching you in the balls.

# I Just Want to Be Alone

**Eric:** I'm stoked about my BJ.

*CLICK.*

**Eric:** Where are you?

**Me:** I'm at the ball punching gloves store getting special gloves for punching you in the balls. Are you kidding? I just talked to you ten minutes ago. You know where I am.

**Eric:** It was more like thirty minutes. Why are you taking so long?

**Me:** Stop calling me.

**Eric:** Nic I'm serious, there's no mayo. I can't wait for my beeeeeeeeee jaaaaaayyyyyyyyy!

**Me:** We have mayo! LOOK FOR IT. I can't wait to punch you in the baaaaaaalls.

**Eric:** MAYONNAISE!

**Me:** BALL PUNCH!

**Eric:** BLOW JOB!

*CLICK*

**Me:** OH MY GOD WHAT NOW?

**Eric:** BLOW JOB!

*CLICK*

**Me:** If you call me again, I'm going to punch you in the balls regardless of the mayonnaise situation.

**Eric:** BLOW JOB!

*CLICK*

**Me:** I'm pulling in the driveway. Please get out here and help me carry in the groceries.

**Eric:** Yeah! Because then I get my blooooooooooow joooooooooob!

*CLICK*

**Eric:** Take a look around, Sweet-tits. No mayo.

**Me:** Hmm … so weird. I could have sworn … hold on a sec.

I GO OUT TO THE GARAGE AND CHECK THE GARBAGE AND FINDS MAYONNAISE IN THE TRASH.

**Me:** Wow. This is a new low. You threw the mayonnaise in the trash.

**Eric:** I did. I wanted a blowjob.

**Me:** You threw out perfectly good mayonnaise. I would have given you the blowjob! What's your problem?

**Eric:** Well, right now my problem is that I'm probably not getting a blowjob.

**Me:** Probably not. At least you have mayo.

# I Just Want to Be Alone

*NICOLE KNEPPER is a Licensed Clinical Professional Counselor whose blog,* <u>Moms Who Drink and Swear</u>, *became the basis for her first book,* Moms Who Drink and Swear: True Tales of Loving My Kids While Losing My Mind. *Nikki, or the "Queen of Cussin," as she is known to her fans in the social media, is known for her commitment to using her vast and diverse audience to raise awareness and funds for charitable organizations. Her unique style of writing weaves common sense, healthy psychology, and humor into her off-color, profanity laced blogs and stories. This honest, nothing topic is ever off limits approach to writing about the hilarity and heartache of parenting consistently draws in new readers, and has resulted in a large and army of loyal readers who identify themselves proudly as fellow moms who drink and swear.*

## Love a Broad
## By Kim Bongiorno
### *Let Me Start By Saying*

Let me tell you a little story about love.

Once upon a time there was a golden-haired girl who met a boy with eyes so beautiful that looking in them was like swimming through a warm summer sky and a cool green meadow all at once.

She knew from the first time they shook hands (not a euphemism) that he was The One, then spent a little time living in sin with him before they tied the proverbial knot.

The lovebirds were quite different from one another, but in complimentary ways. Their adoration made older married couples vomit in their mouths, and children squeal, "THAT is DISGUSTING" when they'd canoodle on the couch during family gatherings. Together they had a dream of a long marriage, a couple kids, and to one day be able to travel around the world together.

Turns out there's nothing like realizing your dreams to marry happily and breed for putting the brakes on international travel. But come their tenth wedding anniversary, they were able to finagle a ten-day second honeymoon across Europe. They both looked forward to how easy it would be to travel without kids, to take advantage of the romance of European cities with no curfew, to fully relish in each other's company with light and happy hearts.

After an epic transatlantic flight and a few hours killing time in early-morning London until their room was ready, the happy couple optimistically skedaddled on over to their first hotel. Longing for a little personal space to freshen up before heading back out into the city for the day, they accepted the room key at their trendy hotel, turned on their smartphone's flashlight apps to navigate their way down dark hallways filled with disco balls, for apparently "abandoned roller rink at night" is all the rage these days, and entered the closet they'd call home for the next few nights.

That's when they realized that they just paid top dollar for a hipster cardboard box. The padded walls made them suspect that a crazy person designed the layout, but it wasn't until the fiber-loving bride had to release her bowels in a tiny echo chamber three feet from

187

her husband while they both pretended he couldn't hear the effects of airplane food that she thought *Hm, we might need to actually put a little effort into the "romance" part of this trip.*

She pushed her way out of the fart amplifier—which had no lock —and swung herself into the coffin-sized shower next to it. The bright lights and mirror were so distracting that she didn't realize the end of the stall was simply frosted glass that looked into the main room. But she became very aware of this design flaw when her pasty bottom was smushed against it as she bent to shave her legs. That did nothing to help put her best proverbial foot forward on the first night of her romantic vacation; her finest feature was absolutely not the one she sits on.

Like witnesses to a mafia crime, the loving couple pretended neither of them saw or heard anything, and ran from Hipster Hotel as fast as they could to walk side by side, taking in the sights, wondering why everyone seemed so much younger than them.

Their visit was full of highs—riding the London Eye, seeing Jane Austen's handwritten notes, and eating meals so delicious they were practically sedatives. It was also full of not-so-highs—slamming a hand in a door, walking down a dark alley in which a local chap might have been smoking crack, and *oh my God jetlag.*

Touring London as nearly-forty-somethings was a little different than she had imagined. Sure, she had a charming fellow on her arm who encouraged her to shop with him, and every new sight was an exciting delight, *but when did her knees start to ache like this?* And why did she wear such uncomfortable shoes?

After a few days, they dashed to the Eurostar for their next destination: Paris, where even a four-hour wait in line for the Eiffel Tower elevators in the heavy summer heat with swollen, blistered feet couldn't hamper the thrill of being there together. They kissed nine hundred feet in the air, while France stretched out around them into a sea of whitewashed buildings with ropes of tiny green knots hugging each neighborhood.

Something about the altitude of the Eiffel Tower inspired her handsome husband to commit to climbing everything within sight. Was it old? Climb it. Were there at least two hundred steps? Climb it. Were the steps steep, uneven, and collapsing before your very eyes? Climb it twice, my friend!

Slick with sweat, she grinned and bore it when he suggested "Hey, let's walk up two hundred eighty-four steps to the top of the *Arc de Triomphe!*" because he was cute when he got like that. Little did she know that after soaking up that view and managing not to tumble back down all those steps, he'd want to walk just a little longer—maybe another forty or sixty minutes or so—to a famous steakhouse for dinner.

Tired and hungry, thoughts began nibbling at the corner of her head, ones like *Does he no longer believe in taxis?* and *He knows I'm a vegetarian...right?* As soon as they turned the corner to see a line twenty people long, she threw an *Aw hey-ell no* look her betrothed's way, marched over to a stone wall, and read a book while he baked in the early evening sun waiting their turn to get a table.

Luckily for him, the vegetarian menu was a personal bottle of wine, cheese platter, and French fries: the Trifecta of Joyful Tummy, as far as his wife was concerned. Her foul mood dissipated like an uninspired storm cloud, and they raced to see who could eat the most in one sitting.

Just like in London, they laughed off the bumps and relished in the French-speaking ride, even though they barely understood a word around them. A few hours in line at the Lourve didn't taint the smile on his lips as he brought her in to see things he knew would thrill her. Rain only made the gargoyles on Notre Dame seem more alive as they photographed every ornate carving, brilliant glass window, and sweeping stone arch around them.

At beautiful Montmartre there was another sweaty hike up endless sweltering steps to the Sacre-Coeur Cathedral, but once they turned around at the top, the view swept them off their weary feet. After a quick coffee and argument over where to eat, they happened upon the street artist from whom her husband had bought a painting for her a decade ago. The coincidence made their eyes shine and fingers intertwine, ready to head off for their next location.

# I Just Want to Be Alone

Until it was time to go to Rome.

Later that evening, in the loud, confusing airport, a cranky attendant told the bone-weary bride that her luggage was too heavy. Sure it was, what with it being packed full of gift-shop tchotchkes and soccer balls (why, husband? WHY?) that her soul mate insisted must be lugged across the continent. So lug, she did: she created a makeshift carry-on with her pillowcase right there in front of all the posh Parisians and elegant Italians.

This is how she found herself storming behind her husband on the most romantic trip of their lives with a lumpy pillowcase stuffed with books over her shoulder and a murderous expression on her face. As they walked in and out of the half-dozen shops between check-in and their gate, he refused to "allow" her to purchase a rolling bag to put *her* crap in, which had been displaced by *his* crap. With each hushed, inexplicable "not here" her anger grew hotter and more irrational. So she punished him by refusing to let him carry the heavy pillowcase that was painfully stabbing her in the back (this made total sense to her, obviously). By the time they had trekked to the gate, her head swirled with thoughts such as, *Who the hell is this man to make me travel like a Depression-era hobo?* La bella vita, *my ass.*

Nary a word was spent between them as they waited to board the plane. And nary a word would be exchanged between them on the plane. Not because she bit her tongue out of anger, but because they were seated separately. She was crammed into her aisle seat by the toilets on the bumpiest flight of her life. As the ladies next to her spilled boiling hot tea from a smuggled thermos across her lap, she yanked grubby shoes off her throbbing feet and thought, *I'd rather deal with these burns than sit next to "No-Bag-For-You" for the next two hours.* She might have even considered throwing her shoe at him—not that there's any evidence on the matter.

But anger can't beat worry. Soon the plane took some dangerous dips, and her heart pitched in his direction; he isn't a fan of flying. She worried, *Is he okay?*

Dizzy from the turbulence and hung over from a bout of intoxicating unfounded anger, she lurched toward him after deplaning to make sure he was all right, and was relieved to see he was. She sated her hunger, and her desire to preload some toots for what would undoubtedly be another tiny, no-lock-having hotel toilet, with a FiberOne bar. He collected their bags, and they took the kind of taxi ride that makes you cling to the one you love and remember to update your will.

And so their love story continued.

Early the next morning, they walked to a shoe shop near their hotel; she slipped on new orthopedic sandals and remembered what it was like to feel happiness again. The couple was wowed by the Colosseum, moved by the Vatican, and overjoyed on a day trip into picturesque Florence. While there, he insisted on climbing yet another two hundred fifty steps up into a crumbling tower, but this time she didn't even hesitate in her decision to race him to the top, laughing all the way.

You see, love and once-in-a-lifetime romantic vacations are a lot alike: you think that once it's set in motion you're guaranteed smooth sailing.

*But, oh, my darlings, it's much more complicated than that.* There's no way to survive—or enjoy the journey—without a little effort and understanding.

Sometimes you'll think the tall and crumbling monuments are breathtaking.

Other times you'll want to spit on the old, collapsing stairs when no one is looking.

Sometimes you'll catch a glimpse of your husband's cheek lifting the way it does when he smiles, and a feeling of gratitude will wash over you, leaving tears in your eyes.

Other times you'll find yourself in a Parisian airport clutching a filthy pillowcase full of your belongings thinking, *If we make it to the next stop without my committing homicide, then this marriage has a good chance of lasting forever.*

And you're probably right.

I Just Want to Be Alone

*KIM BONGIORNO is an <u>author</u>, <u>freelance writer</u>, and the award-winning blogger behind <u>Let Me Start By Saying</u>. Her essays have been published in multiple best-selling humor anthologies, her book* Part of My World: Short Stories *has a solid five-star rating, she was selected as a 2013 BlogHer Voice of the Year, she recently completed her first YA novel, and she manages to do all this while writing regularly for a variety of websites, including Nick-Mom, InThePowderRoom, Mamalode, and* The Huffington Post.

*Kim lives in New Jersey with her handsome husband and two charmingly loud kids. Learn more on <u>KimBongiornoWrites.com</u>, or find her any time of day on <u>Facebook</u> and <u>Twitter</u>.*

# Romance is Overrated
## By Jen
### *People I Want to Punch in the Throat*

"Romantic" is not a word that many would use to describe either myself or the Hubs. We love each other madly and we have no problems showing one another how much we love one another. That being said; my idea of romance is the Hubs folding laundry before I do it, and he would find it romantic if just once I would initiate our "special" time rather than begrudgingly agreeing to get naked after saying, "No" the previous three nights so I could read a book instead.

Recently I overheard one of those annoyingly blissful couples retelling the story of their engagement. It involved a blindfolded limousine ride to a five-star restaurant, a multi-carat ring in the bottom of a champagne glass, and a professional photographer to document the entire proposal just in case someone ever has nothing to do and would like to peruse the photos of this blessed event. The woman was so positive her man was going to pop The Question that night that she'd gone out and bought a new dress and had her hair professionally coiffed. All I could think was, *Good thing she was right or that could have been awfully embarrassing – and expensive if she cut the tags off that dress.*

I'm way too much of a control freak to be blindfolded, and I think Outback is a fancy meal so a five-star restaurant would be completely wasted on me. I am so oblivious to my surroundings that I would have choked to death on my engagement ring if it were at the bottom of a champagne glass.

So while this sounded like a lovely engagement, mine was nothing like it. Instead of limousines, champagne, and paparazzi, mine went down more like a hostage negotiation.

The Hubs and I had been happily dating for several years, but one day I'd had enough. I was twenty-nine years old, and I wanted to know if I wasting my good eggs on him. "What are we doing?" I asked during a commercial break of some stupid sitcom we were watching.

"Waiting for the show to come back," he replied, stuffing his mouth with a handful of potato chips.

"No. What are *we* doing?" I clarified. "Where is *this* going?"

My question was met with dead silence, except the sound of the Hubs slowly crunching his chips.

He swallowed carefully. "I've told you before. I can't get married until I get some things crossed off my list." The Hubs had an extensive bucket list that he wanted to complete prior to marriage. Several of the items were doable, like "Go bungee jumping," but many were just outrageous. For instance, "Win an Oscar," "Save one million dollars," and "Climb Mount Everest" were three in particular that were giving him a lot of trouble.

"I don't mean to be harsh, but I don't think you're going to win an Oscar anytime soon. We have to take that one off the list," I said, crushing that dream like a bug.

"Fine," he agreed, reluctantly. "But what about money? I have no money. I can't get married if I don't have any money." This was true. The Hubs was broke. After graduating from New York University Film School, he'd maxed out his credit cards making a feature film that was supposed to win him an Academy Award or at least a mention at Sundance or Cannes or something, and then make enough money to pay off his debt and then some. Unfortunately, those bastard judges didn't even give his film a chance. They made it incredibly difficult to win when they didn't even allow him to submit his film. I can't say that I blame them, though. His film doesn't exactly scream "box office sensation" to me either. His movie centers around three different generations of non-related women waxing poetic on their lives set to a forlorn musical backdrop. It *is* a bit of a yawner, but not in an artsy fartsy way, just a sleep-inducing way. However, I've always thought the plot would be great for a porn film. I think he just needs to splice in some hot scenes of girl on girl action and change the music to a *bow chicka wow wow* soundtrack, then he could release that shit on the 'net and make bank. He doesn't like my ideas. Whenever I mention this plan to him he goes on and on about "artistic integrity" – as if *I* know what that means!

"The money thing is a bit of a problem, but I think we could make it work. We just need to find a cheaper city to live in," I said.

"Like Hoboken?"

"No. Like Kansas City."

Chips sputtered out of his mouth. "What?"

"I'm ready to go back. I'm so done with this place. I was ready to pack it in last week when that homeless guy on the subway kept pushing his boner against my butt every time the train jostled. I don't think I can take another day like that."

"I told you, the next time that happens, you need to find a different car."

"I'd just moved into that car because another guy was taking a piss in the corner of the car I was just in! That's why the boner guy's car was so full and I was wedged up against him. Everyone was trying to get away from the pisser."

"Well, just ignore those guys. They'll find someone else to harass."

"That's just it. I don't want to ignore someone in the hopes they don't harass me. After a long day at the office, I don't want some homeless guy's boner grinding on me. I keep fantasizing about commuting to work in my own car – alone – and living on a cul-de-sac. I want to move back to Kansas. Last night I dreamt about grass and lawn mowers! I feel like I've had a good run here. *We've* had a good run. It's time to shit or get off the pot."

"You want to get married."

"Well, I don't want to keep dating until we're forty. I love you. You love me. I'm not sure what's stopping us – besides your list. We've talked through every single 'what if' that we could come up with."

"Have we, though?" He finally put his chips down – this conversation was getting serious! "What if I get hit by a bus and I can only communicate with blinks? I'm able to live like that for several years, but my quality of life deteriorates. I decide to give up. One day I blink 'Kill me.' What do you do?"

"I smother you with a pillow and put you out of your misery – because I love you."

"Right. Good answer! However, don't forget to double-check that 'Kill me' is what I'm really blinking. I might have forgotten our code and I could *think* I'm blinking 'Feed me.'"

"Will do! OK, your turn. I'm in childbirth with our third kid. Things are going south. We're both dying. The doctor says he can only save one of us. Which one do you choose?"

"Ugh. I hate this one. This one sucks. There are two kids at home who need their mother more than they need another baby brother or sister, but I know if I choose you, you'll kill me and then our kids will be fatherless. So I choose the baby and then I let your mother raise the kids for awhile while I mourn. Eventually I marry the hot nanny I hire with your life insurance money."

"Hmmm … OK. As long as she loves our kids like her own, you can marry her."

"Yeah, except I don't want to get married."

"OK. Then stay a lonely widower. I like that idea better anyway. It's more romantic. No one can fill my shoes, blah, blah, blah."

"No. I don't want to get married *to you*."

*Ooof. Ouch. Pass the damn chips, maybe they can fill the hole you just made in my heart.*

When he saw me shove chips in my face, he continued quickly, "That didn't come out right. I mean, I want to marry you. *Eventually.* I'm just not *ready* right now. I love you. You know I do. But I'm not ready to get married."

"I see." I put the chips down. I'd rather eat my feelings with chocolate. "Well, I can't spend any more time waiting for you to get *ready*."

It was true. I'd put in several years at that point and I was ready for the next step. Of course, I wanted to take the next steps with this guy, but I wasn't going to beg or try and force him to do something he didn't want to do. I wanted a house and kids and a planned community with award-winning public schools where I didn't need to be on a waiting list before I was even pregnant. If he would rather scale Mount Everest than share a Costco membership with me, then good luck to him. I wasn't going to wait any longer.

"Sorry, Jen." He left in a hurry.

I got out a pint of ice cream and I called my mom and told her it was over. I was positive I'd never see him again.

Luckily my mom didn't say, "Oh thank God! I *knew* this would happen! We never liked that asshole and you can do so much better! Such a shame you wasted four years of your life on a loser!" because the next day my phone rang bright and early.

It was him. "Sooo … What are you doing today?" he asked casually.

*Uhhh … we totally broke up last night, dummy. What is your damage? Why are you calling me?*

"Most likely burning photos of you and opening up an eHarmony account. Why?"

"I wanted to see if you wanted to go shopping."

"For what?"

"Diamonds. You're so damn picky, I can't just pick a diamond that I like. If we're going to do this, we might as well admit right now that you're a control freak and that means picking out your own engagement ring."

"I thought you weren't *ready* to get married."

"I wasn't ready last night. But I thought it through. I'm ready *today*. I'm just a little scared, but I know it's the right decision. We belong together. Even if we have to be together in Kansas. Are you still moving to Kansas?"

"Yes."

"Super! I've always wanted to live in Kansas."

I ignored his obvious sarcasm. "How are you going to pay for the ring?"

"I'll figure out something," he replied.

"What about your list?"

"We can do those things together. You want to climb Mount Everest too, don't you?"

"God no! Do you even *know* me?"

"Haha, of course I do. You'd die on that mountain."

"So would you, you idiot."

# I Just Want to Be Alone

"No, remember? I got that North Face coat at the outlets last winter! The tag says it's totally Mount Everest-rated. And if nothing else I'll just hire some sherpas to carry me to the top. So ... what do you think? Want to go shopping today?"

I was silent. The fact that he wanted to go diamond shopping made my stomach feel queasy (I'm sure all the chips and ice cream the night before didn't help either), but because I'm an asshole, I couldn't say that, so instead I snapped, "Oh all right! Just come and pick me up."

And so we went shopping, because he was right about the diamonds and my desire to control everything. He wanted to get a pear shape. *Ugh. As if!* I am a square cut girl all the way. Plus, I was able to keep an eye on him and make sure his idea of "figuring out something" didn't mean slipping in a cubic zirconia stone when no one was looking.

Sure, he's a cheap bastard who can be a tad anti-social and a bit of a know-it-all, but he treats me like gold, so he's my lobster. We might not be the most traditionally romantic couple, but our relationship works for us. We've built the foundation of our marriage on relentless teasing of one another, constant griping, and the knowledge that no one else could possibly stand us, so we'd better make this work.

Oh wait. I forgot about love.

I meant to say the foundation of our marriage is love – love of bickering.

*Jen is the blogger throwing hilarious punches peppered with a liberal dose of f-bombs on her blog* People I Want to Punch in the Throat. *Jen is also the publisher and editor of* I Just Want to Pee Alone. *She is the author of* People I Want to Punch in the Throat: Competitive Crafters, Daycare Despots, and Other Suburban Scourges *and* Spending the Holidays with People I Want to Punch in the Throat. *She has been featured on* The Huffington Post, Babble, *and* Headline News.
*She is wife to The Hubs and mother to Gomer and Adolpha (not their real names – their real names are actually so much worse).*

# NOTES FROM THE EDITOR

Are you all done? Are you looking for more? I've got some good news for you. First of all, this book is volume two in a series. Have you read volume one, *I Just Want to Pee Alone*? Well, what are you waiting for? Go get that book right now. And B, every single lady writer in this book has a lot more to say. Please be sure to find us on the web where we have blogs with tons more to read, and many of us have additional books on Amazon. You can also follow us on Facebook, Twitter, Pinterest, G+, Instagram, and whatever new and improved social media exists at the time that you're reading this.

Thank you for reading this book. We appreciate your support. We had a great time putting this together. If you liked this book, please tell all of your friends, your family, your hair stylist, and the lady behind you at Target who looks like she could use a laugh. When you're done telling the world about this book, please leave us a review on Amazon, because those reviews are crazy helpful.

If you hated this book, I'm sorry and *Namaste*.